BLUE SUEDE BROGANS
Scenes from the Secret Life of Scottish Rock Music

JIM WILKIE

MAINSTREAM
PUBLISHING

Edinburgh and London

ACKNOWLEDGMENTS

This book is dedicated to Caroline Sweeney of St Andrews. It would not have been possible without the co-operation of the interviewees and I thank them all.

Thanks are also due to John Ruggieri, Michael MacNaughton, Sandy Jones, Shug and Carol, Keith Harris, Duncan Henderson and Grace Maxwell. Love to Lorna and Eoghan.

Photographs came from a variety of sources but, principally, the Glasgow Rock Garden archive, which, I believe, was largely the work of Alan Fullager. The resources of the Mitchell Library, Glasgow were also utilised.

Unfortunately, not everyone I would have wished to talk to was available for interview. Alex and Les Harvey, for example, two brothers who made a tremendous impression on the Scottish scene, died prematurely. Hamish Stuart and Maggie Bell live abroad and Annie Lennox was taking a year off to have a baby.

Jim Wilkie
August 1991

Copyright © Jim Wilkie, 1991

All rights reserved

The moral right of the author has been asserted

First published in Great Britain 1991 by
MAINSTREAM PUBLISHING COMPANY (EDINBURGH) LTD
7 Albany Street
Edinburgh EH1 3UG

ISBN 1 85158 372 6 (paper)

No part of this book may be reproduced or transmitted in any form or by any other means without the permission in writing from the publisher, except by a reviewer who wishes to quote brief passages in connection with a review written for insertion in a magazine, newspaper or broadcast

A catalogue record for this book is available from the British Library

Typeset in Fournier by SX Composing Ltd, Rayleigh, Essex
Printed in Great Britain by Butler & Tanner Ltd, Frome

EPIGRAPH

'Henry (Stallings, a friend from his youth in Georgia) was a lot more country than we were – he wore overalls instead of jeans, and his shoes were *brogans* (author's italics) . . .' – *James Brown, in his autobiography, The Godfather of Soul.*

Brògan is the Gaelic word for shoes and Georgia was one of the American states which was initially colonised by Scots Gaels, as opposed to the Lowland Scots or English. One party in the 1780s was said to comprise mostly Gaels from around Inverness, and it is in the Highland capital, a century later, that this story begins . . .

JAMES BROWN

*ELECTRIC CEILIDH
BAND*

JIM WILKIE was born and educated in Dundee. His school band was called the HALOS (1963-66) and, after University and a move to Skye where he co-founded the *West Highland Free Press*, he toured extensively with DOG EAT DOG (1972-74). Following a brief stint with SHUG BARR'S ALLSTARS (1975-76) he signed a publishing deal with Island Music in London, recorded an album – *The Waxer* – with Scottish musicians including CADO BELLE (1979) and toured with the Dundee MAFIA (1980).

With the ELECTRIC CEILIDH BAND (1979-) he has recorded some Gaelic crossover material and has appeared in a number of television programmes including BRAG (BBC Gaelic TV) for which he also acted as Music Producer.

He was featured in a Wildcat Channel 4 special – *Bless My Soul* – and one of his songs, a political satire, was recorded by BILLY CONNOLLY.

BLUE SUEDE BROGANS is his third book.

CONTENTS

PROLOGUE

TAJ MAHAL is the adopted name of the black American singer, Henry Sainte Claire Fredericks-Williams, although to describe him as a 'singer' would be like calling Harlem a 'suburb'. His work is a living musicology which simultaneously brings a sense of history to popular culture and explores new avenues for Afro-American music; his influence has been enormous. His RISING SONS group featured the young Ry Cooder; he recorded with the POINTER SISTERS when they were in their early teens; he rescued Mississippi John Hurt from terrible obscurity, prior to Hurt's death; his work influenced the BLUES BROTHERS project. The list is a long one.

In the spring of 1980, Taj made a rare appearance at the Rainbow Theatre in London and, such was my interest, I rearranged a metropolitan visit to coincide with the event. Unfortunately, my companion pulled out at the last minute, but I felt I was bound to know someone in London who was going to see Taj Mahal – and so it proved – although, by the time I had hung about the 'George Robey' and then the foyer bar for an hour, I was slightly inebriated. The bell rang and I headed for my seat. A steward stopped me at the auditorium door and, as I fumbled for my ticket, I began to hear the familiar, plummy tones.

'Look, don't you see?' an elegant, though somewhat desperate, female voice was pleading to an impassive doorman. 'We *had* our tickets when we came through the main door, but now we appear to have *lost* them!'

I looked up, and my ears had not deceived me. 'Josephine . . . ,' I said.

She didn't recognise me at first, and was obviously with someone, but as the second bell rang he had begun to melt into the distance.

'Jim Wilkie!' she enthused, preparing to clutch at straws. 'How are you? Look, Jim, we *had* our tickets but we've *lost* them.'

Now, if this had happened a few years earlier and it was fire-walking we were about to undertake, I would have been unlacing my shoes. I was slightly older now but, as a result of my alcohol intake, not much wiser.

'Look,' I said to the bouncer, holding up my ticket and somehow pretending she was now with me, 'she obviously had a ticket or she wouldn't have got this far.'

It was some understatement, that.

Anyway, to my surprise, the guy let us through. We were soon joined by her boyfriend – six-feet-four, aquiline features – and they both shook my hand warmly.

9

TAJ MAHAL

'How marvellous!' exclaimed Josephine. 'You must phone me, for lunch.' I'd heard that before.

Elated, I made my way down the aisle, just in time to see Taj coming on to the stage. He went straight into *Cakewalk Into Town* and, in my delirium, I found myself joining in on the chorus.

'Well I'm feelin' so much better, I could cakewalk into town!' I sang at the top of my voice.

'SHUT UP!' roared a mob of blues students in unison. They were probably all dressed the same as well. You couldn't see in the dark. I crawled into Row F.

Taj finished the first song to a great reception. He must have been disconcerted by a crowd shouting 'Shut up!' at the end of his first chorus but, having

LONNIE DONEGAN
ROCK GARDEN

composed himself, he began to talk. The voice was like a honeyed version of Louis Armstrong's.

'Aaah, thaink y'all,' he drawled. 'Ah'd juz lak t'say that it's great t'be heeuh, in Englan.' Polite applause. Ah yes, the blues. 'Y'see, Englan' always bin impo'tant t'me see, ma mamma an' daddy, they'd sang *Freight Train* you know, Nancy Whisky? Yeh.'

Although partly stupefied, I was able to register that this was an interesting fact. *Freight Train* was actually written by a black American woman, Elizabeth Cotton, and it was curious that Taj, of all people, should remember Nancy Whisky's version.

'And then,' he continued, 'then records came into the house by that cat, Lonnie

Donegan. Yeh? Yeh?'

A bolt began to move slowly down the back of my head and spine, making me sit up in my seat. Taj Mahal listened to Lonnie Donegan when he was young?

'Yeh, Lonnie Donegan. You know, them Leadbelly songs?'

Good grief, Lonnie Donegan introduced Taj Mahal to Leadbelly?

'Now,' said Taj, 'the fact that Lonnie Donegan was *English* . . .'

I had never done this sort of thing before, but I was sitting quite near the stage, and I just had to stop him.

'Eh, Scottish,' I piped up.

The crowd around me fell silent. A football hooligan. I was exposed, but there was no way back.

'Eh, Lonnie Donegan was Scottish, actually.' My voice was tailing off in embarrassment, but this was important, because I always believed the Scots have a special affinity with black music.

Taj Mahal by this time must have been wondering what the hell was going on but, as a scholar and gentleman, he paused for a moment to give it some thought. The crowd held its breath.

'Yeh?' he said, finally. 'Yeh? SKADDISH?' He paused again. 'Uh, ah didn' come heeuh to offend nobody.'

Laughter and wild applause burst the atmosphere. Taj was saved. The concert was saved. Even that clown in Row F was saved. Amen!

'She caught the Katy
Left me a mule to ride . . .'

INTRODUCTION

To many Americans, and to musicologists in particular, Scotland represents a unique treasure store of Gaelic song, Scots ballads and Norse fiddle tunes. Conversely, Scots have long had an ear for American music but something remarkable happened in the years which followed the Second World War. Young Scots in unprecedented numbers began to desert their own musical heritage in favour of a new American popular music hybrid called rock'n'roll.

Essentially a black form, one of the most cogent explanations of its origins has been given in separate circumstances by the veteran (black) soul singer JAMES BROWN and LEVON HELM, the (white) drummer with a Canadian group, THE BAND. Rock'n'roll, they have asserted independently, grew up in the south-eastern states of Tennessee, Georgia and Alabama, Louisiana, Mississippi and Florida, because of the tradition of travelling shows, circuses and medicine shows which incorporated authentic black artistes in a way that vaudeville theatres did not. There was also a parallel northern development of electric rhythm and blues, particularly in black Chicago, but the first 'stars' tended to come from the south and that great rock'n'roll original, LITTLE RICHARD, was performing in medicine shows as early as 1950. It is not difficult to imagine how the application of outrageous show business techniques to the delivery of black, gospel-based music gave the seminal rock'n'rollers their style and potency. When this was then taken on board by white country singers like ELVIS PRESLEY, the EVERLY BROTHERS and JERRY LEE LEWIS – whose tradition suggests that Scots/Irish music was the other major component part of rock'n'roll – then adopted by the globally-powerful American media, the international success of the new music was assured.

In Scottish showbusiness at this time, there was also a divide. Variety theatres presented vaudeville Scottish music in the style of Harry Lauder alongside comedians and the occasional British or American 'crooner,' while more authentic Scottish country dance music was played at village halls and ceilidhs, or at dance halls and ballrooms in tandem with popular British and American dance music. Folk song was underground.

The early Fifties, however, was a time of musical revival in Scotland. Scottish folk song was brought to the attention of a wider public by academics and singers like Norman Buchan, Ewan MacColl and Hamish Henderson and traditional New

Orleans jazz became popular, again particularly with the younger generation.

It was from this trad jazz scene that LONNIE DONEGAN emerged. Born Anthony Donegan in Glasgow in 1931, he moved to London as a child and was a guitar and banjo player with Ken Colyer's Jazzmen when he adopted the Christian name of American blues singer, Lonnie Johnston, and began performing 'skiffle' – guitar-based folk and blues music – as an interval attraction with the band. Donegan then teamed up with Chris Barber, enjoyed British and American chart success in 1954 with LEADBELLY'S *Rock Island Line* (his fee was £3.50) and became Britain's most successful recording artiste prior to CLIFF RICHARD with his 'do-it-yourself' skiffle music, which young people could and did try to copy, often using washboards and tea-chests as primitive instruments.

The only other Scot to have hit records in the mid-Fifties was Jimmy Shand. His country dance band became internationally famous and, in spite of their low-key, homely image, were capable of generating such interest that policemen were occasionally required to disperse crowds which clamoured for admittance to their dances. Such an incident outside a club in Cricklewood in London was described by *Melody Maker* as a 'riot'.

Music-inspired riots became much more commonplace throughout Britain with the arrival of rock'n'roll: riots at concerts, riots in cinemas when rock'n'roll films were shown. There appeared to be something liberating for young people about this music and even some of the places that one could hear rock'n'roll properly (that is loudly) carried an element of danger – carnivals and funfairs which were situated on the rough, no-man's land of towns and cities.

The Scottish contribution to rock'n'roll has rarely carried danger. It has, however, continued to be characterised by these two, early strands: some variation on what is generally perceived as traditional 'Scottish' music, and a particular identification with black or Afro-American forms which other British and European countries either did not aspire to or did not achieve. Some English musicians in the late Sixties (ERIC CLAPTON, ROLLING STONES, PETER GREEN, etc) managed to forge successful links with the blues but it has not been sustained in the same way that Scots groups have continued to hold faith with soul music, over decades, and generations.

The Irish, it might be said, have also moved between black and traditional styles and have to date been the more successful fusionists in the instrumental and English language areas (VAN MORRISON, MOVING HEARTS). It may be that the Celtic peoples share traditional musical values with their African counterparts – a liking for quality voices, dancing and instrumental virtuosity (which, in America, has also found expression in jazz) – and whereas the Celts in Ireland and Scotland have perhaps identified secularly with the blues and its rock offspring, the Lowland urban Scots have found more resonance in the 'churchy' singing styles and harmonies of soul music. Certainly, the churches held a more central role in people's lives in Scotland in the Fifties than they do today, and city churches have traditionally been places of social gathering for displaced persons, whether they come from the Highlands of Scotland, Ireland, the southern states of America or Africa.

Scots have figured in the UK charts quite consistently since the Fifties, but in small numbers. Such statistics, however, do not tell the full story. It is obvious that one cannot get hit records if one cannot get major record deals and if Scots have to travel to London to find studios and major record companies in the first place, the odds against their work being understood, never mind appreciated, are quite significant. Perhaps more significant, however, is the fact that Scots have done better in each succeeding decade since the war. There has been a slowly developing music business infrastructure in Scotland (studios, promoters, etc) and there are portents of meaningful musical fusion. Could it be that Scotland is poised to emulate the success of England in the Sixties, Jamaica in the Seventies, or even Ireland in the Eighties?

Just as there has been a mixture of musical styles, there has also been a dichotomy of professional life in Scotland, for whereas the Scottish media has tended to concentrate on UK charts and Scottish artistes famous in a British context, there has also always been a distinct, professional rock scene in Scotland which sustained itself through local work. Indeed, the concept of being a 'working band' - a band which sounded competent live and could replicate its records – is an important one in the Scottish context. By the time the next batch of 'Scottish' hits appeared, in the late Fifties and early Sixties – LORD ROCKINGHAM'S ELEVEN, JACKIE DENNIS, CLYDE VALLEY STOMPERS, ANDY STEWART, KARL DENVER – there were a number of 'serious' Scottish rock groups which enjoyed a (Scottish) national reputation. These groups did not have access to ballrooms or even, in some cases, municipal dance halls. Instead, they would tour the miners' welfares of the central belt or the village halls of north-east Scotland. In 1960, the most significant of these groups was the ALEX HARVEY BIG SOUL BAND.

Alex Harvey was born in Gorbals, Glasgow, in 1935 and achieved wider celebrity in 1956 when he won a newspaper competition to find 'Scotland's Tommy Steele'. His musical interests encompassed a much wider range than the pop charts, however, and, fuelled by imported records – like Steele, at least one member of his

KARL DENVER
ROCK GARDEN

band had been a merchant seaman bringing home records from the US – he established the BIG SOUL BAND in 1959, the first British band to assume a 'soul' identity. The band was slightly exotic among the younger groups in that it featured the saxophone and a black conga player. It played throughout Britain and Germany, where it made an interesting connection with Dundee contemporaries, the POOR SOULS. The two cities – Glasgow and Dundee – were to provide a 'soul axis' which would become important in the wider world of popular music.

Latterly, the BIG SOUL BAND also included Alex's younger brother, Leslie, a first-class guitarist who was later to make a name for himself with the R&B group STONE THE CROWS, featuring MAGGIE BELL. Alex himself enjoyed a reprise in the 1970s with the SENSATIONAL ALEX HARVEY BAND but, tragically, both he and his brother were to die prematurely – Leslie from electrocution on stage and Alex from a heart attack in his early 40s. Their influence on and importance to the development of the Scottish rock music scene is inestimable.

16

MAGGIE BELL
ROCK GARDEN

LULU
242 MAGAZINE

By the early Sixties a distinctive Scottish pattern was beginning to emerge. The BEATLES were the most important influence – curiously the north-east of Scotland was one of the few places where they were able to put tours together before their international breakthrough – but Scottish interest in soul music and rhythm and blues was also developing rapidly and, in 1964, Scots achieved hit records in each genre. LULU (b. Marie Lawrie), whose longevity in showbusiness now rivals that of CLIFF RICHARD, had a top ten smash with the ISLEY BROTHERS' song *Shout* and fellow Glaswegians, the POETS, who affected a Rabbie Burns image, scored with an original R&B-style ballad, *Now We're Thru*. The group was managed by Rolling Stones' manager, Andrew Loog Oldham, and vocalist George Gallacher almost secured a unique double when he was later considered as a footballer by Jock Stein's Glasgow Celtic. Many young Scots boys, of course, played both football and music but few achieved such prestigious attention in both.

By the mid-Sixties, every Scottish town had its soul music scene and

17

FRANKIE MILLER
ROCK GARDEN

accompanying 'Mod' fashions. When an archetypal English Mod group such as THE WHO toured in Scotland, they would be supported by two or three Scottish soul groups. The Who themselves would have been influenced by black dance records but, whereas the English groups had begun to strike out with their own material by this time, the Scots tended to stay more loyal to the black originals. Indeed, one Scots vocalist who was beginning to cut his musical teeth around then – FRANKIE MILLER – was later told by Otis Redding's widow that she had never heard a voice so close to that of the great man; also the (new) POETS enjoyed a second wind in the late Sixties as a 'covers' group alongside other favourites of the period like the

18

CHRIS McLURE SECTION, the BEATSTALKERS and the PATHFINDERS – all West Coast groups which were popular throughout Scotland.

During this period of 'national apprenticeship' in Scotland, the international scene was transforming. The BEATLES had opened up a world market for new 'English' music often with European rather than Afro-American pretensions and the ROLLING STONES entered a highly creative period of original rhythm and blues. A number of Scots-born musicians – Ian Anderson of JETHRO TULL, Jack Bruce of CREAM, DONOVAN and the INCREDIBLE STRING BAND among them – made significant contributions to developments during this period but there was little which was identifiably Scottish about their work and, in any event, the English media was too wrapped up in the English idea to notice, and what weight it carried was thrown behind a plethora of bizarre and bizarrely-named English groups too numerous to mention, or even remember.

The result was that Scots were largely confined to the margins. We had our own hippie groups – BEGGARS OPERA, WRITING ON THE WALL, BREAD LOVE AND

THE
BEATSTALKERS
ROCK GARDEN

CHRIS McCLURE
ROCK GARDEN

19

JACK BRUCE

Left: STRING DRIVEN THING ROCK GARDEN

Right: BEGGARS OPERA ROCK GARDEN

DREAMS, STRING DRIVEN THING – and folk rockers quick to pick up on the Fairport Convention idea (JSD BAND), but pop success came only with MARMALADE or Opportunity Knockers' LENA ZAVARONI and NEIL REID (talent shows always seemed to hold a fatal attraction for Scots).

It was not until the mid-Seventies that we were getting a more serious piece of the action although, even then, serious money was only going behind 'image' groups like the BAY CITY ROLLERS or SLIK (featuring MIDGE URE) who were being manoeuvred by Scots Svengalis Tam Paton and Frank Lynch from Edinburgh and Glasgow respectively. Then a brave, albeit costly, managerial initiative worked for Dunfermline hard rock group, NAZARETH, and ultimate artistic/commercial credibility finally arrived with the AVERAGE WHITE BAND.

The White Band was an amazing phenomenon. A mix of Dundee and Glasgow soul musicians, they had moved to London and worked without

commercial success or even artistic recognition until a fortuitous meeting with Jerry Wexler took them to the classic soul music Atlantic label. Their first album for Atlantic topped both the US mainstream and (black) R&B charts simultaneously – the first and only white group ever to achieve this – and the group members continue to have distinguished individual careers.

For most Scots at this time, however, the American route was not a realistic option. There had to be London success first and some quality artistes were at least 'bubbling under'. The remarkable HUMBLEBUMS folk group produced both a comedian (BILLY CONNOLLY) and songwriter (GERRY RAFFERTY) of international standing; STONE THE CROWS had two great black voices in MAGGIE BELL and JIMMY DEWAR and they had unearthed another fine guitar player in JIMMY McCULLOCH from Greenock; BENNY GALLAGHER and GRAHAM LYLE continued their songwriting odyssey which had carried them from Ayrshire to the Beatles' Apple Publishing, then from McGUINNESS FLINT to their own performing band; and BARBARA DICKSON, from Dunfermline, completed her transformation from folk singer to pop star. In Scotland itself there was outstanding new soul talent in CADO BELLE from Glasgow and CAFE JACQUES from Edinburgh, although neither group made it into the charts.

Another revolutionary development in youth culture was soon to turn the music scene upside-down, however. The advent of punk, in 1976 – anarchistic fashion and musical thrash – was to have important implications and specifically for young Scots as new-wave independent record labels were now as likely to spring up in Larkhall as in London, and Glasgow notched up a quick success with the idiosyncratic Postcard Label and its prodigious stable of ORANGE JUICE, JOSEF K and AZTEC CAMERA. Then came mainline chart success from the SKIDS and the REVILLOS, bands with Fife connections but very different musical styles. And eventually – inevitably, some would say – Scots began to crack it right across the board. There was massive, international success in the Eighties for the EURYTHMICS and Aberdeen-born ANNIE LENNOX; SIMPLE MINDS (who were also managed by a home-based Scot, Bruce Findlay) looked set to take over the international GENESIS market; then a whole range of good Scottish artistes, most with obvious black influences – BIG COUNTRY, JIM DIAMOND, DEACON BLUE, WET WET WET, DANNY WILSON, HUE AND CRY, THE WATERBOYS, LOVE AND MONEY, BIG DISH, EDDI READER, TEXAS, JIMMY SOMERVILLE, DEL AMITRI, LLOYD COLE AND THE COMMOTIONS, and the BLUE NILE – began regularly to find chart positions. Oh yes, and Andy Stewart had a revival of *Donald Whaur's Yer Troosers?* Some media habits die hard.

It was the novelty of Scottish artistes establishing themselves artistically and commercially in identifiably Scottish idioms, however, which to my mind was

SLIK ROCK GARDEN

*Far left: GERRY
RAFFERTY* ROCK
GARDEN

*Left: BARBARA
DICKSON* ROCK
GARDEN

23

*Left: RODDY FRAME
(AZTEC CAMERA)*
ROCK GARDEN/PETER
ANDERSON

*Right: THE
WATERBOYS*
CHRYSALIS RECORDS

perhaps the most significant development of the Eighties. The group RUNRIG from Skye had waged a successful guerrilla campaign on behalf of Gaelic music to become arguably the greatest phenomenon in the history of Scottish rock music and like the PROCLAIMERS from Auchtermuchty, began to get chart positions in uncompromised Scots voices. And songwriters like MICHAEL MARRA from Dundee were managing to bring American and Scottish styles together in original, sophisticated and identifiably Scottish ways.

This, then, is a history of Scottish pop/rock/blues/soul music. It is not a conventional history, as I have not always felt compelled to follow charts or famous people, the usual rock indicators which are frequently neither reliable nor interesting (to me at least). Instead, I have chosen to speak to a variety of people – Scots – whom I respect for different reasons. I have tried to present them in their own words so that any future historians will have more than my imagination to go

on. And by speaking to people from different *eras* as well as diverse *areas* of Scotland I would hope to establish the fact that there is such a thing as a distinct Scottish tradition in rock music, albeit one which hovers spiritually somewhere between Dundee and Detroit, Skye and the southern states of America.

What *Blue Suede Brogans* seeks to do is examine some of the processes which have brought us to this point: the collective experience of Scottish musicians and others, famous or otherwise, which constitutes the (hitherto) secret life of Scottish rock music.

Right: JIMMY SOMERVILLE WITH BRONSKI BEAT ROCK GARDEN/ PETER ANDERSON

Left: THE BLUE NILE ROCK GARDEN

25

LATE NIGHT DANCE

BEAT BALLAD SHOW
Presenting
Star of TV and Decca Recording Fame—
JOHNNY GENTLE and HIS GROUP,
Supported by Scotland's Own Tommy Steele—
ALEX. HARVEY and HIS BEAT BAND,
With Ballad Singer—Babby Rankine.

To Entertain and Play For
DANCING
in the
TOWN HALL, ALLOA,
on
FRIDAY, 20th MAY,
9.30 — 1.30.
ADMISSION—Before 10 p.m., 4/-: after 10 p.m., 5/-.

Buses After Dance to the HILLFOOTS DISTRICT.

NEXT FRIDAY, 27th MAY — JOHNNY DOUGLAS
and HIS NEW BEAT COMBO with Happy Jackie
Benson and Andy Cook of S.T.V.

Another winner from Northern Border Dances :-
The Beat Ballad Show, presenting Star of T.V. and Decca
recording fame, **Johnny Gentle** and his Group, supported
by **Rikki Barnes** and his All Stars with Lena and Stevie, to
entertain and play for dancing in the **Town Hall, Forres,**
on THURSDAY, 26th MAY, 9 p.m. to 1 a.m.

Admission 5/-
Please Note Free Buses will leave Farraline Park Bus Station at 8 p.m. via Ardersier,
Gollanfield, Regal Car Park, Nairn, to Forres.   Returning after dance

CHAPTER ONE

ALBERT BONICI

The North East

'Henry (Stallings, a friend from his youth in Georgia) was a lot more country than we were – he wore overalls instead of jeans, and his shoes were *brogans . . .*'
– James Brown, in his autobiography, The Godfather of Soul.

'*Brògan*' is the Gaelic word for shoes and Georgia was one of the American states which was initially colonised by Scots Gaels, as opposed to the Lowland Scots or English. One party in the 1780s was said to comprise mostly Gaels from around Inverness, and it is in the Highland capital, a century later, that this story begins.

In 1892, a 16-year-old Italian immigrant named Giuseppe Bonici arrived in Inverness from his home in the northern Italian town of Burgo Val di Taro. He had travelled north and west on the prospect of employment by a Scot who owned two businesses in the town, a shop/cafeteria and a newsagent's. Giuseppe could speak neither English nor the Gaelic which was, of course, the common linguistic currency but in spite of this he was immediately put in charge of the newsagent's shop along with a junior member of the Scottish family.

The short-term solution to the language difficulty was typically pragmatic of the immigrant. A large board was found on which every item the shop sold could be written in English and Gaelic, while on the reverse, the same information could be found in Italian. Such determination was to take Giuseppe far in business. By the time he was 24 he had bought the newsagent's and, prior to the outbreak of the First World War, he had added the cafeteria, plus another café in Union Street, Aberdeen, on a site which is now occupied by the Capitol Cinema. As an Italian national he was compelled to go back to the country of his birth for the duration of the war, and he married in Italy. He returned to Inverness, however, and it was in that town that his eldest son, Albert, was born in 1920.

Albert Bonici was an intelligent child who inherited his father's interest in languages. He was educated at St Joseph's College in Dumfries and the family would holiday alternately in Scotland and Italy. As luck would have it, the outbreak of the Second World War found Albert and his mother in Scotland, while his father, younger brother and sister were in Italy, and this precipitated a move to Elgin, where a cousin had a business – the Park Café.

'We felt at home both in Scotland and Italy. My parents were reunited after the war and both died in Elgin. I did an engineering course at various universities including

Opposite: JOHNNY GENTLE AND THE SILVER BEATLES, ALLOA 1960
COURTESY: KEN BEATON/JOHN ASKEW/ PAVILION BOOKS/MARK LEWISOHN

ALBERT BONICI
ALBERT BONICI

London during the war, and I worked in that capacity for a few years. But it seemed just to happen that I came into the family business, in 1952.'

Before long, Albert was to strike up a friendship which was to change the course of his life.

'I used to pay 2s 6d a week to a Murphy's pools agent, who filled out the coupon. One week, I won a few hundred pounds – which was quite a lot of money – and it made me feel uneasy. I decided to cancel the coupon and a young journalist named Henry Robertson who worked on the *Elgin Courant* got to hear of this. He was a good musician who had been to university but had developed TB and was writing newspaper articles while he recuperated in Elgin. We became good friends and to help him raise money to stage the music shows which he put on in local church halls, I organised a Valentine's Day dance. It made a fair bit of money.

My wife and I were keen dancers, but we had to travel to the Northern Meeting Rooms in Inverness to see the big bands, because they only did the major centres. The circuit was something like: Monday, Edinburgh Palais; Tuesday, Dundee Palais; Wednesday, Beach Ballroom, Aberdeen; Thursday, NMR Inverness; and Friday and Saturday, Green's Playhouse in Glasgow. No one wanted to know about Elgin.

My brother-in-law had a connection with Tito Burns, the London agent who handled the Ray Ellington Quartet, and Burns said Ellington would come up if three venues could be found. There was still a great demand for dancing at this time so it was not a terribly great risk. The big bands toured once a month so I put the Ellington Quartet in between visits. They did the Beach Ballroom on a Wednesday, the Assembly Rooms, Elgin, on a Thursday, and Forres on a Friday. It was a big success.'

In fact, this tour was to put the north-east on the map as far as popular music was concerned and for the next 20 years or so, many of the small towns in Moray, Nairn, Banff and Buchan were to enjoy a feast of British and American music.

Henry Robertson, meanwhile, had taken up residence with Albert's sister in London and, again through Tito Burns, made a useful contact with Chappell Music and the actor/singer, Jim Dale. Before long he was auditioned by Jack Good and, as Musical Director for the legendary *Oh Boy!* television show, he became *Harry Robinson,* the leader of Lord Rockingham's Eleven, which proceeded to score a major hit with *Hoots, Mon!* a big band version of the traditional *One Hundred Pipers* into which Robinson would call, 'Hoots, mon, there's a moose, loose, aboot this hoose!' It appeared that the memory of Harry Lauder was still very much alive and still bankable.

In Elgin, Albert Bonici's music promotions continued to develop. 'I made contact with the trad jazz agent who handled Kenny Ball – a Canadian session musician named JACK FALLON – and in time, we did a lot of business with his Cana Variety Agency. We took two or three chart-topping roadshows such as EDEN KANE and KARL DENVER *(a Scot whose real name was Angus MacKenzie)* to Aberdeen and the Dundee Caird Hall, and this gave us an insight into the world of touring concerts. We had an office with eight people, and links with other promoters such as Andy Lothian in Dundee and Duncan MacKinnon in the Borders. By the early Sixties we had established a circuit for our own bands such as JOHNNY AND THE COPYCATS *(later a recording band)* and the JACOBEATS, both of whom came from Buckie. It was something like: Tuesday, Fulmar Club, Lossiemouth; Wednesday, Keith, Dingwall or Nairn; Thursday, Elgin; Friday and Saturday, Cullen and Buckie in the North, or Kilmarnock and Stevenston in the South; and Sunday, the Beach Ballroom, Aberdeen, for which we had a contract. Added to that were other forces' venues and university dates. Two bands would be playing at the same time and crossing over.'

By the early Sixties, Albert Bonici was Scotland's principal pop music promoter. Working bands were earning £30 per night and chart groups could be offered a slightly more lucrative five-day tour. Albert also opened his own ballroom in 1960, the Two Red Shoes, behind the Park Café in Elgin. Within three years, it was to have some extremely distinguished visitors.

MY DEAR WATSON
(formerly Johnny & the Copycats)
ALBERT BONICI

The BEATLES had played in Scotland before, in May 1960 when, as the Silver Beatles, they had backed a Larry Parnes singer named Johnny Gentle. This was their first professional work and the tour encompassed Alloa, Inverness, Fraserburgh, Keith, Forres, Nairn and Peterhead, with Borders promoter Duncan MacKinnon hiring the halls. MacKinnon complained about the scruffiness of the group which comprised Lennon, McCartney, Harrison, Stuart Sutcliffe (who was born in Edinburgh) and a drummer named Tommy Moore, and they were paid £10 each per week.

Jack Fallon had also previously encountered Brian Epstein and, just prior to the Beatles having their first hit (*Love Me Do,* in November/December 1962), Fallon and Bonici contracted the group for what was seen as a routine five-day tour, to commence on New Year's Day, 1963. It would seem that Mr Epstein, however, omitted to read Albert's small print.

'London was very unsophisticated about Scotland. They looked upon it as a unit, like Liverpool, so when we inserted a clause into the contracts requiring all groups who wished to return to Scotland to do so under our auspices, no one took any notice. They simply signed the contracts.'

Brian Epstein signed Jack Fallon's contract dated 9 November 1962, committing the Beatles to five nights in Scotland at £42 per night (probably £40 plus £2 booking fee). The venues were Keith (1 January 1963), Elgin (2nd), Dingwall (3rd), Bridge of Allan (4th) and the Beach Ballroom, Aberdeen (5th), and the group was to fly into Aberdeen direct from Hamburg which they had reluctantly agreed to visit over Christmas 1962. It was a particularly bad winter, however, and the flight was delayed, thus depriving the good citizens of Keith their (second) place in pop history. The next four gigs were negotiated successfully, however, and Albert looked forward to his usual Monday report.

'I was a jazz man and didn't really listen to the pop groups much. On the Monday, I travelled to Aberdeen Station and was picked up by my associate, Gordon Hardie. We went as usual to Chivas Restaurant in Union Street, only this time we were surrounded by waitresses clamouring, "Who are these Beatles?" The group had apparently visited the restaurant earlier in the day and made a great impression. I don't know if it was their personalities or the smart blue suits and raincoats into which the name "Beatle" was sewn, but they had certainly impressed the girls, and that made an impression on me.'

Opposite: BEATLES CONTRACT, 1963
ALBERT BONICI

Five days later, the Beatles made their first appearance on the influential ITV pop programme *Thank Your Lucky Stars,* and within six weeks they were

CONTRACT 1908/

Cana Variety Agency

(BANDS : CABARET)   (JOHN P. FALLON)   GERard 0227-8-9

5 Wardour St., London, W.1

LICENSED ANNUALLY BY THE L.C.C. ———— MEMBERS OF THE AGENTS' ASSOCIATION LTD

This Agency is not responsible for any non-fulfilment of contracts by Proprietors, Managers or Artists,

An Agreement made the ....9th.....day of ......November...19 62

between .....A.A. Bonici Esq.,..............................hereinafter called the Management

of the one part, and .....Brian Epstein Esq.,.................hereinafter called the Artiste

of the other part.

Witnesseth   that the Management hereby engages the Artiste and the Artiste

accepts an engagement to present.................**T H E   B E A T L E S**...................

(or in his usual entertainment) at the Dance Hall/~~Theatre~~ and from the dates for the

periods and at the salaries stated in the Schedule hereto.

The Artiste agrees to appear at   **five** ~~one~~   Evening performances

at a salary of £...42.0.0. per date Percentage terms...........% Guarantee £................
    (forty two pounds)

SCHEDULE

five Day(s) at Scotland, venues to be advised   on 2nd - 6th Jan.   19 63

.............Day(s) at ....on ....19........

ADDITIONAL CLAUSES

1. It is agreed that.......................———.............................shall appear in person.   (at

2. The Artiste shall perform for a maximum of.......**one hour**............divided into ...**2 x 30 minute** (each
   sessions commencing not earlier than....**to be advised** and terminating not later than..**to be advised** (venue
   at times by arrangement between Management and Artiste.

3. The Management shall provide first-class amplification, microphone equipment and piano in good condition tuned
   to concert pitch.

4. Financial settlement for this engagement shall be made with .....~~£/¢/£~~ Brian Epstein Esq.,
   on conclusion of the tour.

5. The Management shall supply the Artiste or his representative with full facilities to check gross receipts throughout the evening and a full accounting of same at the conclusion of performance.

6. The Artiste shall not, without the written consent of the Management, appear at any place of public entertainment xxxxxxxxxxx in Scotland xxxxxxxxxxxxxxxxxxxxxxxxxxxxxxxxxxxxxxxxxxxx
   xxxxx prior to xxxxxxxxxxxxthis engagement.

7. The promoter agrees that any other band performing the engagement(s) described in this agreement shall be
   composed of members of the Musicians' Union, and in the event of Musicians' Union action arising from the
   engagement of non-unionists the promoters shall be responsible for payment of the full fees or percentages as
   stated in this agreement.

8. The Artiste(s) to wear Uniform dress.

9. It is agreed that should the Management not confirm this engagement within 10 days of the date of the issue of
   this agreement, it shall become null and void.

10. The Management to have the first option to present this attraction in Scotland
    following this booking.

11. Full publicity material to be sent direct to:
    A.A. Bonici Esq., 7, North College Street, Elgin, Morayshire.

Signature ....

Address .....Nems Enterprises Limited,....
        12/14, Whitechapel, Liverpool 1

number one in the British Charts with *Please Please Me*. By the spring, the major London promoter, Arthur Howes, was trying to place them on a Cliff Richard concert in Glasgow, but he had not reckoned with the contractual awareness of Albert Bonici. An interdict was served on Howes, and new terms were confirmed with Brian Epstein for future Beatles' Scottish appearances on the basis of a gentleman's agreement.

Albert Bonici went on to present the Beatles in two further Scottish tours. In October 1963 they appeared at Dundee, Glasgow and Kirkcaldy, for a fee of £300 per night and in October 1964 they played in Glasgow and Edinburgh for £1,000 per night.

Albert carried on with this type of business until the mid-Seventies, promoting the KINKS, SEARCHERS and ROLLING STONES, among others. His 'special clause', however, was coming under closer scrutiny, particularly when the solo group concert (pioneered by JETHRO TULL, he believes) came into vogue. He recognised that the days of the controlled tour were numbered. In 1975, he turned the Two Red Shoes into a freezer centre and built a hotel on the outskirts of Elgin. He remained a gregarious and cosmopolitan figure, who recognised that he might have made more money had he moved his operation, even to Glasgow. But he was not complaining. 'Elgin,' he said, 'is a nice town.' He died in 1990.

THE TWO RED SHOES BALLROOM, ELGIN
JIM WILKIE

CHAPTER TWO

Glasgow and the West

'They liked rock'n'roll *(in Glasgow)* long after everyone had progressed to liking the Shadows . . . I suppose they haven't got much else to do up there.' – *John Lennon, 1963.*

Perhaps it is to be expected that the Second City of the Empire, hub of the tobacco trade and great Atlantic seaport which Glasgow has been at different times in its history, should have strong links with the USA and its music. So it has proved. In the Thirties and Forties it was said to be the dancing capital of Europe and, with a keen eye also for American fashion, there was traditional affinity with American 'front' or "gallusness" – the brashness which gets you noticed.

Inasmuch as Scots have 'made it' to any degree in pop music, Glasgow and Glaswegians have been there or thereabouts, and yet the city was a relatively late developer. There were a number of individuals – LONNIE DONEGAN, KARL DENVER, ALEX HARVEY, JACK BRUCE – who made early headway and also one or two successful bands – the CLYDE VALLEY STOMPERS *(Have Tartan Will Trad)*, BIG SOUL BAND, BIG SIX – but when the BEATLES exploded on the scene in 1963/64, a *Melody Maker* survey revealed that whereas there were thought to be 350 groups in existence in Liverpool, Glasgow was said to contain only 12! Further, it actually named ten of them – SOL BYRON AND THE IMPACTS, the SAPPHIRES, the APACHES with Tommy Scott (later Dean Ford), JOHNNY LAW AND THE MI5, the CHAPERONES, the FLINTSTONES, the KINNING PARK RAMBLERS (Leslie Harvey's Group), the CHARIOTS, and JAY ANDERS AND THE CHEVRONS – and estimated they were playing to approximately 2,000 people per week for approximately £100 per band. Clubs listed were Lennoxbank Sunday Club, Teenage Mansion, Maryland, La Cave, and the Lindella in Buchanan Street, where Lulu was first spotted. By May 1964, LULU AND THE LUVVERS were the first Scottish beat group to chart. They reached number seven with the Isley Brothers' song *Shout*.

ALEX HARVEY'S BIG SOUL BAND was described in the same publication (along with Newcastle's ANIMALS) as 'one of Britain's few authentic R&B bands' and, in 1964, they recorded a single of *I Just Wanna Make Love To You*, the Muddy Waters song which the Stones had popularised on their first album. By November of that year the POETS, who were managed by Andrew Loog Oldham (Rolling Stones' manager), had a hit with an original composition *Now We're Thru* and it was felt in some quarters (not for the last time) that Glasgow might be the next big thing. Unfortunately, it was a claim which would not achieve substance for many years.

JIMMY GRIMES

'How would you like to get into debt?

Jimmy Grimes was the bass player in the ALEX HARVEY BIG SOUL BAND. A former merchant seaman, he continued to play folk and blues after quitting the group, but his first love is the sea and he now devotes much of his spare time to small boats.

'I was born in 1934 in Glasgow, at Janefield Street in Parkhead and I stayed there until I was about 30 although I went to sea. My father was a Catholic from Donegal and my mother a Protestant from Belfast. My interest in music would have come from them . . . My father would sing lovely old Irish songs like *The Boston Burglar* or *The Croppy Boy* when he came in at night. He was a miner in Lanarkshire. I've got three brothers and three sisters . . . I'm the youngest.

I was interested in music from the age of ten or 12 and singin' songs like *The Three Caballeros*. My first introduction to an instrument was when I was in the Merchant Navy about the age of 19 *(early Fifties)*. A guy came aboard the ship and had a guitar. I bought it off him for a pound . . . and a loaf! Ah gien him a loaf an' that clinched the deal! I think his name was Smith and he came from Shetland. He taught me the five chords which, he said, got him through every song in the world!

At school there was maybe a piano but otherwise I never saw an instrument. It was songs like *Mr Froggy Goes A Courtin'*. The first records I liked were by Frankie Laine . . . *Jezebel* and *The Girl In The Wood*. At that time, though, there were no opportunities. There were a series of halls like the Parkhead Public and the guy who ran the local bicycle shop had a band – BILL LATHAM AND THE MELODY MAKERS. There was Parkhead Public, Tollcross Co, Shettleston Co, the Brigton Public – public halls which some entrepreneur would hire to hold a dance. Jamie Barnes was playin' at that time.

Basically, of course, we went to fight. It was somethin' to do on a Saturday night. We would go up an' if you didn't get some female to go home wi', the next best thing was a battle. You looked around to see who came fae Shettleston an', equally, if you felt a bit bold, then maybe three or four of us would go to Shettleston. You would always end up gettin' chased. There was a runnin' two-minute battle before too many of them arrived on the scene. You might get a punch in, then it was through closes, over walls and across fields.

I went to the Merchant Navy when I was 17. The option was military: go to Kenya and kill somebody in defence of somebody's plantation. The guy from Shetland taught me a song called *Fifteen Years Ago Today* by Jimmy Rodgers – the Singin' Brakeman – then he taught me more of his songs like *Waitin' For A Train* and he told me that Rodgers was popular in Shetland. So, when I came home, there was a shop in Parkhead – Stanton's in the Gallowgate – which sold aw' these obscure records. It just so happened he had a box o' them that he couldna get rid o', and he sold me the lot for a shillin' each. I got *Desert Blues* and then he pulled out LEADBELLY and LEFTY FRIZELL (1953/54). And MacCormack's, who had a very small shop in Cowcaddens, seemed to be able to get you what you needed, musically.

Now, also at this time, I used to always go campin' an' I run intae a load o' people. There was a lot o' war surplus equipment an' a load o' people took tae the hills at weekends. So I ran into groups of folk like the LAZY Y from Clydebank and the STAG and MICKEY FINN, folk that played guitars and sang when they were campin' at places like Drymen or Luss. Friday tae Sunday, all along the banks o' Loch Lomond you would hear things like *Tumblin' Tumbleweed* . . . beautiful voices, and KARL DENVER – Gus MacKenzie – came out of all this and so did ALEX HARVEY. We were weekend drifters, playin' cowboys for a weekend.

First of all I met a guy called Bobby McGerty whose brother, Jim, was playin' piano wi' a trad jazz band called the McGERTY FIVE PLUS TWO. Bobby took me up to this church hall place in Mollinsburn Street in Springburn where the band was playin' and he says, "There's a wee guy up here you'll no' like. He's got an evil face" *(laughs)*. This was Alex Harvey who was playin' trumpet . . . I think it was *Sweet Georgia Brown*. He had a wee twisted eye which made him look a bit strange, but it turned out I got on okay with him. He lived in the Gorbals and his mother was a lovely wee woman. His father was quite left-wing but I don't think they were musical. Alex had learned a few chords from a couple of guys who had guitars in the Gorbals.

I met him, probably, in 1955. I was at sea and I began to bring him records – I brought him the *Big Bamboo* from Blackbeard's Tavern in Barbados, calypso records, and others from other places. We both liked blues and work songs – *Dark Is The Dungeon* – and if I heard somebody singin' one of these songs, I went out of my way to learn it. He was a couple o' years younger than me and one weekend we were away campin' and he had to leave early for this contest to find Scotland's Tommy Steele. He won it and became a kind of celebrity.

Now, PRESLEY had happened by this time, but it was LONNIE DONEGAN who really impressed me. I went to get BURL IVES singin' *John Henry* and the guy in the shop didn't have it but said that it was also a Donegan B-side. And the A-side was *Rock Island Line*. I thought, "Jesus, this is powerful!" Donegan really swung. He came originally from Glasgow but he grew up in London and I had no knowledge of him. I probably mentioned him to Alex but he needed no introduction. It was the same later when I first let him hear BOB DYLAN.

So, I was still bringin' back records and magazines – cowboy magazines where PRESLEY was 'The Country Cat' – and Alex formed a band when I was at sea. Charlie Carsware, Willie White, Bobby Rankine ... some from outside the town. They played around Glasgow and the outskirts and later we went to Inverness and even Wick, which was a 14-hour drive at that time *(1960)*. We also went to Orkney and Shetland.

After Alex won the competition he was appearing in four different places in one night plus people were goin' out *as* Alex Harvey. Joe Moretti told me he did it once in Armadale ... guys were holdin' up photies ... and one who had a cuttin' said, "You're no him, ye ken." Of course, he couldn't admit it for, as he said, "If ever they fun' oot in thae wee toons, they'd a ripped me apart!" Dangerous business.

After seven years at sea I got the sack. I was always in trouble ... missin' boats ... and I had no time for authority. I had started off as a deck boy, sailin' in a converted MacBrayne boat – the old *Hebrides* – which was an old tub an' we used to tie her up to tree stumps. Sometimes in the islands people would row out in boats an' pass up sheep tae us, one at a time. I ended up an AB *(Able Seaman)* and a British AB had a good name, so I was considering the Norwegian Merchant Navy.

Anyway, I was at home and Alex came across and his words were: "How would you like to get in debt?" He said I could have a job wi' the band but I'd need to get an instrument. I said okay. If someone else had come along an' asked me if I wanted to go on an Antarctic expedition I would a said yeah.

I got an acoustic guitar first because you couldn't get a bass guitar at that time *(1959)*. A year later I got a Fender Jazz bass and it was the only one in Glasgow. An English band had got into trouble and sold it to MacCormack's. It was just another piece of paper to sign! Stuff like money never changed hands in them days! They took me to court but eventually the bass became mine.

Alex had great tonsils. He was a powerful singer and he wrecked guitars by twisting and bending them when he played. His guitar playin' was weird. He just wanted to succeed whereas it didn't matter to me, and he didn't want trouble whereas Hoagy *(sax)* and myself would sometimes get involved. He could carry a lot on his wee shoulders though an' he could handle a crowd. He seemed to know what to say and what the crowd wanted.

The BIG SOUL BAND played at La Cave club in Midland Street with a trad band called the STEADFASTS. We did one night a week . . . me, big Wally, *(a Jamaican conga player who had joined in somewhere along the line),* and 'Hoagy' Carmichael, George MacGowan *(drums)* and a couple of singers, Bill Patrick *(brother of Bobby)* played sax before Hoagy and he gave the band the name. I think it was the first soul band in the country. Then we started doin' a lot of work with Larry Parnes and his teenage idols . . . Vince Eager, Johnny Gentle, Marty Wilde, Dicky Pride. Dicky Pride was really good and, in 1960, we ran into the BEATLES. We normally did a weekend wi' the singers . . . Armadale, Sauchie, Rosewell, Inverness – mostly miners' welfares an' town halls . . . an' I think we were comin' back from somewhere when we met the Beatles in Alloa. They were called the Silver Beatles and they wore black gear. Also, they used four guitars . . . they didn't have a bass and were interested in mine although, as I recall, we didn't actually play wi' them. They didn't make much impression on me either.

We did a lot of work at this time. In one 24-hour period we did six jobs, La Cave then down to Alexandria, back to Glasgow, then on to an all-nighter at a club in Leith Walk in Edinburgh wi' ANDY FAIRWEATHER. Then La Cave twice again on the Sunday. Even wi' aw the pills – purple hearts that women could get on prescription for slimming – you still fell asleep. Andy Daisley was the manager for a wee while. He was a lamplighter from Baillieston but Alex seemed to manage to bankrupt everybody who tried to help him!

The German gigs came from the guy that ran the Two I's coffee bar in London. He booked us into the Top Ten Club in Hamburg which was a beautiful place and a great experience *(1960).* The POOR SOULS from Dundee were there later and they were great but we never met the BEATLES gain. There were some fantastic people in Germany at that time . . . RAY CHARLES, the EVERLY BROTHERS, BO DIDDLEY . . . and we would be on the same bill. Alex also made an album across there although, for some reason, I wasn't on it.

So then we played in London and the south of England . . . we toured with SONNY BOY WILLIAMSON, BIG DEE IRWIN . . . and Alex's brother Leslie played with us at that time. Beautiful human being . . . but I left soon after that. We weren't gettin' the money we were due from management and after I found that out I didn't fancy carryin' on. But I still got on well with Alex after that.

I came back to Glasgow and just made money doing folk-songs in pubs. Just enjoyin' mysel'. Anythin' I've got in life I just fell over . . . there was never a plan.

The boat was aboot the only thing I wanted and eventually I got a beauty in Rothesay. She had been built for John Hammond Teacher to race J-class by Sir William Fyffe who built the Shamrock boats for Thomas Lipton to race for the Americas Cup. The guy – John Graham – would only sell to me if I promised not to strip the boat. Unfortunately, the Renfrew Ferry stretched her moorings and sank it later but I love boats and I've got another one now.'

THE (NEW) POETS
(Iain MacMillan's
Wedding) ROCK
GARDEN

Left: RONNIE
SIMPSON RONNIE
SIMPSON

Right: (RARE) ZAL
CLEMINSON with BO
WEAVLES SHOWBOAT

CHAPTER THREE

RONNIE SIMPSON

'Mining areas were always creative places'

Ronnie Simpson came through from performing in groups to running Scotland's most successful agency, Music and Cabaret. He is now the managing director of the more traditional Scottish Lismor Record Company.

Born in Motherwell in 1942, Ronnie was originally a singer with a group called the CHORDETTES. *When the group later amalgamated with another to become the* IMPACTS, *Ronnie was moved sideways into the manager's chair.*

'Dancing in the 1950s was run in ballrooms and municipal halls. In Lanarkshire there was Airdrie Palais *(Town Hall),* Coatbridge Town Hall and Bellshill Miners' Welfare; down in Ayrshire you had community centres at Auchinleck and Dalmellington; there were miners' welfares at Shotts and Whitburn – mining areas were always creative places in terms of their musical taste; and there were ballrooms at the Trocadero in Hamilton, Bobby Jones in Ayr, and the Raith in Kirkcaldy *(Fife).* Dances were where people dressed up and bands were 20 or 25-pieces.

I went straight from school into a band. I worked in John Williams in Wishaw which made nails and I was sacked for bad time-keeping. Then I moved to Ravenscraig and the same thing happened. You were working nine to five stampeding down the road, grabbing a sandwich and a bowl of soup, and then off to wherever.

Rock'n'roll was a bit like the punk thing – it wasn't wholly acceptable – so some of the bands started booking community centres themselves. When the main hall crowds started to go down, that's when the first changes started, and rock'n'roll bands then went into all the halls except the ballrooms *(which succumbed later).*

Glasgow was a bit of an unknown quantity. It had lots of ballrooms and people like Johnny Wilson who was a bus operator and promoted wherever he could find halls. There was the Lindella Jive Club which mostly played records; another jive club *(Bill Murdoch School of Dancing)* at the Botanic Gardens; Cuthbertson's Maryland Club in Scott Street; and they also opened the Elizabethan

Club in what's now the Riverside. There were clubs in Lennoxbank and Baillieston, and the Iona Community Centre had the odd thing on the Broomielaw. La Cave is now The Arches and you went in up a close.

My band was playing around Airdrie, Bellshill and Coatbridge. Our first big trip was to the Regal Cinema in Nairn and we thought, "Where the hell is Nairn?" You had to be there by 9.30 and when the cinema closed at ten they cleared out the front row of seats. We had a good reputation up there and were asked back once a month *(from 1959 to around 1961)*. By this time I was the manager so I used to buy the local paper wherever we went. I found the Aberdeenshire *People's Journal,* and then we found Albert Bonici.

Later, for the whole of the Fair, we would play for Bert Ewen, who was a baker in Inverurie – Ellon, Udny, Mintlaw, Peterhead, Fraserburgh. Bert Smith in the Lothians ran Whitburn, Grangemouth and Falkirk. He would always have the bands doing "doubles" like Stenhousemuir and Whitburn, and the last half-hour would be a jam session with the likes of SOL BYRON on the stage with ALEX HARVEY.'

(By then, Ronnie's band had become Sol Byron and the Impacts, and subsequently Sol Byron and the Senate.)

'Sol Byron *(Billy Lockhart)* came originally from Larkhall, and a character in the band I remember from that time was a guy called "Alki", from Tannochside. His great trick was to get pissed on wine and sing Little Richard – screamin', wi' the eyes bulgin'. But then he'd jump off the stage into the audience, forgettin' that he only had six foot of cable on his microphone. Little things like that.

By then I had started hitting on the ballrooms and we would do the JM in Dundee, the Flamingo in Paisley Road West *(Glasgow)*, and the Bobby Jones. The management of the Flamingo was keen on a group called the POETS, and wanted us to let them on at the interval as the Rolling Stones' manager – Andrew Loog Oldham – was coming up to see them. Mr Singleton *(owner)* spoke to him and a deal was apparently arranged. I said, "What about the big band?" "The Poets have an image," said Loog Oldham.' *(It would not be the last time that such a reason would be given for English impresarios passing on certain Scottish groups.)*

'The band that impressed most people around this time was the GOLDEN EAGLES who came from the Bathgate/Whitburn area. They were a seven or eight-piece and run by brothers, one of whom – Brian Johnston – went on to become a member of the Senate group which moved to London. His brother, Bob, would hold out for his money and get, like, £75 when a band price was £20 *(1963/64)*.'

42

PROMOTERS

'We never really worked for him but Duncan MacKinnon was the first promoter to really expand his operation. Although he was based in the Borders, he was running dancing in Wick and Thurso. Perth City Hall was run by John Wallace, but the one who had the best trick was Bill Fehilley. He and his brother ran dances up north and no matter what one of them you got, his brother had the money elsewhere! You had to keep on top of these people for your £35 or £40.

Bill Fehilley later became very big in bingo and, somewhere along the line, he re-discovered ALEX HARVEY. Derek Nicol, who had worked for Andy Lothian, was working for me and Fehilley approached him with a view to "making Alex a star". Derek had his own band, NAZARETH, and Eddie Tobin, who had been managing the BO-WEAVLES, switched them around to become TEAR GAS, then the SENSATIONAL ALEX HARVEY BAND.

It was very much a case of the money making the hits and Bill was the man who created the "buy-on". Previously bands did not pay for support work on tours. Bill made paying for the privilege a national standard.'

> By the late Sixties, Ronnie had progressed from his own agency – Impact, in Lanarkshire – to a city-centre operation, Music and Cabaret, with partner Alex Scott.

'There had been a second generation of clubs in Glasgow – the Picasso in Buchanan Street; Le Phonograph, across the road *(run by Tony Gordon who, until recently, managed BOY GEORGE)*; and a soul club in West Nile Street, run by Joe McCourtney and Alex Scott, who also ran venues in Drumchapel and Easterhouse. Alex had gone on to manage groups like the PATHFINDERS, the new POETS and the DREAM POLICE, whereas I now had the venues, so we formed Music and Cabaret and started booking all the bands constructively around the country. Eddie Tobin and Andy Cumming *(ex-bass player, CHRIS McCLURE SECTION)* were also involved. We ran gigs from Gretna to Strathpeffer and all points east and west. We booked the clubs like Michael McNaughton's Carioca, and the Place in Edinburgh, and were particularly successful in the colleges and universities, but soon everyone wanted to drift south. The assumption then was that everybody had to go to London. The better bands had some success – the PATHFINDERS were signed by the Beatles' Apple organisation; HUGH NICOLSON of the POETS joined MARMALADE; HAMISH STUART went to the AVERAGE WHITE BAND; and Alex Scott himself did well in management, first with YES, then the STRAY CATS and now, with East End Management in LA, he looks after STEVIE NICKS and THE TRAVELLING WILBURYS, among others.'

In the heyday of Music and Cabaret, Ronnie struck up a working relationship with Frank Lynch who then ran the Electric Garden at Glasgow's Mayfair Ballroom, and who went on to manage BILLY CONNOLLY and SLIK (*MIDGE URE et al*). Lynch subsequently refurbished Green's Playhouse as the Apollo Theatre which Ronnie directed for a year ('I named it, and created the full-house award') before moving his operations to Florida. Following a brief and unhappy stint at Shuffles Disco (also at the Mayfair), Ronnie became involved with Lismor Records, the traditional Scottish label which he now runs. He is also Secretary of the embryonic Scottish Record Industry Association.

THE PATHFINDERS
FRASER WATSON

DREAM POLICE
ROCK GARDEN

CHAPTER FOUR

FRASER WATSON

'Their music had that wildness, too. It was part of their soul'

Fraser Watson is a Glasgow musician whose career now spans 30 years. As guitarist with two of Glasgow's most important groups of the Sixties, he was at the forefront of the Scottish rock scene for a decade and enjoyed the patronage of both the ROLLING STONES and the BEATLES. He is also one of the most well-liked players on the Scottish scene.

'I was born in Glasgow in 1947 and after a year on the South Side we moved to the Cleveden Road area of the West End. My father was a one-man business – a builders' merchant – and he also played drums, part-time: jazz, big band stuff, before and after the war.

We always had a great selection of records . . . Nat King Cole, Sinatra, Louis Bellson . . . and I suppose that was the stuff I first liked. I went to Hyndland School and when I was 13 we moved to Blantyre.

I started playing trumpet when I was seven. My dad took me up to the Greens Playhouse ballroom to see the Ted Heath Orchestra and to the Kelvin Hall to see Louis Armstrong. I loved it but the school music lessons were pretty boring and my own kids are going through the same thing at the moment. They play flute and clarinet.

My father then brought home an old cello acoustic guitar. F-holes, no strings on it and his mate was flinging it out. It lay around the house for about six months then I went to Cuthbertson's on the corner of Cambridge Street and Sauchiehall Street and got a set of strings – heavy gauge, tape-wound things that no one could play. I was about 13, I got Bert Weedon's *Play In A Day,* and I was away. There was a lot of music happening, ELVIS, BUDDY HOLLY, EDDIE COCHRAN . . . even CLIFF and the SHADOWS. The Shadows were a great band then . . . the sounds they got out of the old Fenders.

My first band was the ARROWS. It was just a guy I was at school with who was learning drums – George Grant – and two others who had left school. George had a snare drum from the BB, I had an acoustic guitar that I stuck a wee mike on to and played through a reel-to-reel tape recorder. I always had an interest in sounds. The first gig, we had a Selmer 8-watt amp for myself and the rhythm guitar; singer and bass guitar all went through a Philips record player speaker. The drummer had a bass drum, snare, hi-hat and one cymbal which his father had made in his work. Everyone had relations who were engineers or something then.

So we just flung it together. We rehearsed in a basement that we could hardly stand up in. I got a Hofner V2 Strat copy and others just volunteered to play other instruments. It was stuff like *Walk Don't Run, Apache,* and so forth and we took a tape up to the local Youth Club in Kelvindale and they asked us to play. We also met a guy called Dave Stevenson who became our singer *(Dave Hunter)* but on the first night he didn't turn up! So we played seven instrumentals. Half an hour between the table tennis and the records.

The Arrows started by doing covers, then some of our own stuff and we

FRASER WATSON
with LOUIS
ARMSTRONG
FRASER WATSON

BARROWLAND
BALLROOM
NEWSPAPER CUTTING

travelled around quite a bit. I can remember being the guest band at a talent competition in Dundee and seeing ALAN GORRIE in a band *(1964)*. We were the "professional" guests and they were better than us!

47

The music scene was changing quickly then but in Glasgow there was always a great blues and R&B thing. George Grant worked with a guy in an insurance office who didn't play anything but had a collection of 2,000 black American singles. Pre-Motown. There was that kind of interest when people got a hold of something and even in my dad's day he thought that the Scottish musicians had a good feel, like the black players. It was maybe a similar struggle in a way. Something about the warmth of people in spite of hard conditions.

Anyway, there were loads of gigs. Every town and village had its dances and when I was still at school I was working five nights a week ... intervals at the Barrowlands or Maryland, Broomhill Tennis Club, and up north to Oban and Strathpeffer. I wasn't interested in school, particularly in Hamilton which was pretty right-wing in terms of its teachers' attitudes, and that sort of thing affected you. Twice I got six of the belt for having long hair – to my ears – and my father tried to plead my case ... that I wanted to be a musician. But the Head wasn't having any of it. He even stopped me sitting 'O' grades.

But, of course, these were different times. Even if you walked through Glasgow with long hair and a guitar case, folk would shout abuse at you. F— poof! Also there were plenty of jobs available but the objective was *not* to take a job. And my parents always supported me, which was a great thing. It meant I could go for the best gear – Vox AC30 and Strat – plus a decent PA. We worked for some agents ... Andy Currie in Ayr who ran the bases, and John MacGowan who handled Barrowlands.

In Glasgow, DEAN FORD AND THE GAYLORDS *(later MARMALADE)* were a great band. It was a Shadows thing but they were very professional and had a great sound. The BLUES COUNCIL with Les Harvey was another great band. They played at the R&B Allnighters at the Candlelight Club *(Botanic Gardens)* before it moved to West Nile Street and Les also worked in Cuthbertson's for a while. I remember seeing him in the KINNING PARK RAMBLERS with MAGGIE BELL at an audition for German work in Partick Burgh Hall. He was in short trousers and playing Wes Montgomery! He was possibly the best guitarist I ever heard ... although some of the scenes these bands got into were pretty wild. And their music had that wildness, too. It was part of their soul.

So, more of the bands were getting away from the pop thing and into R&B but our guys weren't developing. One had a job, one was going to university and so forth. My mother and sister answered an advert in the *Evening Citizen* – "Professional group seeks guitar player" – and this was the POETS. They were signed to Andrew Loog Oldham *(ROLLING STONES' manager)* and had had a couple of

THE POETS with
George Gallacher
(centre) and Fraser
Watson (bottom left
FRASER WATSON

singles and a minor hit, although I hadn't heard them at this stage.

I went to an audition at the Flamingo Ballroom in Paisley Road West and there were about 50 guys and their friends. I sat outside for an hour, I was so nervous but, when I eventually went in, George Gallacher *(vocalist)* passed me at one point, saw my long hair and said, "If you're any good, you're in!" Meaning the image fitted. I was also surprised by how good they were.

I became a director of the company – £8 a week – we rehearsed three or four times a week at the Flamingo and played all over Scotland and England. There were riots even although the group was slightly on the wane. Everywhere we went in Central Scotland there were four double-decker buses of fans, and it was pretty amazin' because we played some pretty obscure *(blues)* stuff – yet here were aw these lassies from the schemes, goin' for it. For what was the fourth single, we went to London and recorded in the Pye studios. Three songs . . . and it was serious stuff, an afternoon to get the snare sound or bass right . . . and Loog Oldham was the producer. He was good . . . the Poets' stuff had a different sound – in fact, it's getting attention right now from kids in America, England and Europe – but after *Now We're Thru* they got no airplay. There was then a fall-out between Oldham and Singleton who ran the Flamingo and the Poets' Scottish operation and I think Jimmy Savile was the only one to play *That's The Way It's Got To Be,* which I thought was a great single.

George Gallacher and Hume Paton were the main songwriters. George had worked in Clydebridge steelworks with the bass player, John Dawson, and Jim Breakey was the *(second)* drummer. I replaced a guy called Tony Myles. George came from Garngad – a tough background in the East End, and his father was a strong communist – and after the Loog Oldham thing fell apart, George fell out with Hume Paton's father who was a businessman and thought he could run the band. I think there was also a sectarian thing there.

Norrie MacLean *(bass)* and Iain MacMillan *(guitar)* then joined from a Paisley band, the BOOTS, and that eventually moved on to another top-class Poets group *(1969/70)*: MacMillan *(bass)*, Hugh Nicolson *(guitar)*, Johnny Martin *(keyboard)*, and Dougie Henderson *(drums)*. In between times, the fans had gone to groups like the BEATSTALKERS and CHRIS McCLURE.

Meanwhile, the singer Ian Clews who also came from a Paisley band, the SABRES, had passed through another group, the MERIDIANS, with MacLean, MacMillan and the drummer Jeff Allen *(who later went to STONE THE CROWS)* and had ended up in the PATHFINDERS with Timmy Donald *(drums)*, Colin Morrison *(bass)*, Ronnie Leahy *(keyboards)* and Neil MacCormack *(guitar)*. When MacCormack left that group, I joined *(1967)*.

> Author's note: Ronnie Leahy also played in STONE THE CROWS and Norrie MacLean subsequently went to the SCOTS OF ST JAMES, where he was replaced by Alan Gorrie.

George Gallacher, who is now my brother-in-law and a very strong character – bright guy, was a good footballer and so forth – he went to London on a songwriting deal. He was involved with the agent Malcolm Nixon, and Tommy Scott of Major Minor Records who also took an interest in the Pathfinders.

In Glasgow, it was the time of the *(pirate)* Radio Scotland Clan balls and, doing good soul material, the Pathfinders began to move. Some of the early gigs were very tough . . . St Convilles in Pollock, heavy place . . . and you were terrified, but both Clewsy and George *(Gallacher)* could handle things and the young gang leaders actually identified with them.

The Music and Cabaret Agency came on the scene then, and all the groups had to play chart stuff and wear suits or they didnae get any work. This affected a lot of good groups like the STOICS *(Frankie Miller)*. Alec Scott of MAC managed the Pathfinders, but we decided to break from him. Ian had done the first demo of the Marmalade thing, *Lovin' Things,* without the band and there was a bit of trouble.

50

Then some of the other MAC groups like DREAM POLICE and DJs like Tam Ferrie were slaggin' off the Pathfinders in public, but the group stayed popular with the fans. A couple of times we did as many as four gigs in one night – Prestwick, Kilmarnock, Sauchie and the late-night Picasso Club in Glasgow.

We did demos of some of George Gallacher's songs and the former Shadows drummer Tony Meehan who was helping George, picked up on the band. We went to London in the summer of 1967 and spent a month there, starving. We were, in fact, often saved by Shuggie McGinley who ran Glasgow's Ram Jam Club. He was down in London and would liberate food from supermarkets!

Anyway, Tony Meehan paid for some demos and eventually *The Road to Nowhere (CAROLE KING)* emerged as a possible single. One night, we were sitting in the Cromwellian club, totally depressed after a rotten gig, when Tony came in and said "Apple – the Beatles' record company – want to release it!" It was like a dream.

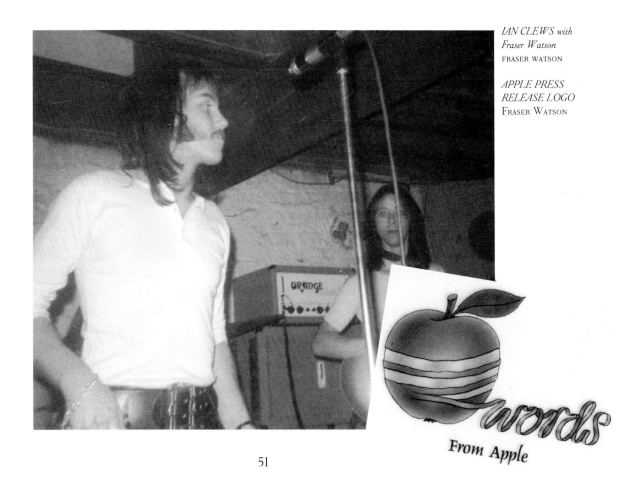

IAN CLEWS with Fraser Watson
FRASER WATSON

APPLE PRESS RELEASE LOGO
FRASER WATSON

SHUG BARR
(centre, guitar) with
NORTHWIND
SHUG BARR

Of course, the reality was different. *(See* The Longest Cocktail Party, *Charisma Books, by Richard di Lello.)* The songwriter, Lesley Duncan, released *Road To Nowhere* before us, then there was the controversy over the new group name WHITE TRASH – and by that time the Apple thing was beginning to fall apart. We had a fair bit of contact with GEORGE HARRISON and I later played on his first solo album but LENNON and McCARTNEY had fallen out and sometimes things were pretty terrible. We spent a lot of time in the Press Office with Derek Taylor though, and he got us an early copy of the *Abbey Road* album to try and get a single.

We chose *Golden Slumbers* and got some of George Harrison's solo studio time. Derek was happy but the Beatles had to be consulted and at least two of them had to agree on any project. George Harrison was away somewhere, Ringo agreed but McCartney didn't. So we were sitting in the office with our reception all set up waiting for a reply from Lennon. Yoko took the thing to him, then came back and said, 'Okay. It's going to be released.'

That kept us going for a wee while but there was a kind of Apple backlash going on in the media and we didn't get to do *Top of the Pops*. White Trash carried on for a couple of years. We toured with MARSHA HUNT who was Jagger's girlfriend at the time and we were supposed to be in the 'Stones in the Park' concert, but she pulled out a couple of days before. We would have done all right there. We were a solid working band.

52

There were a few more changes. Noddy MacKenzie from Inverness came in on guitar and there was another deal with Essex Music, but I wasn't part of it.

I got an offer to join SWEET . . . Brian Connolly was from Blantyre and knew of me . . . but it wasn't my thing and I toured for a while with a group called CUPID'S INSPIRATION. Then I teamed up with Hamish Stuart and Matt Irvine *(DREAM POLICE)* and Willie Munro *(RITE THYME)* in the BERSERK CROCODILES and we had interest from the Black Sabbath producer, but there were lots of fall-outs and I ended up coming back here.

I started my first job when I was 28 – and was labouring for four years. I played with SHUG BARR and then teamed up again with George *(Gallacher)* in the DEAD LOSS BAND *(1975-early Eighties)*. We were managed by Jack Irvine of Scottish tabloid fame and he got us some publicity, but there were no records. Then there was a disastrous studio investment and it took the next band, the DANSETTES, to pay off the debt. That led to JIVE ASS *(bigger, rock'n'roll combo)* and now I've got my own wee studio in Busby.'

DEAD LOSS BAND
M8

53

GRAHAM LYLE
PETER DAGELEY.
RONDOR MUSIC

54

CHAPTER FIVE

GRAHAM LYLE

'When we got to the chorus, I said, "Try singin' What's Love Got To Do With It?"'

Graham Lyle is one of Scotland's outstanding musical exports. He formed a song-writing partnership with BENNY GALLAGHER in Ayrshire which then moved to London and the Beatles' Apple publishing company. Their next band, MacGUINNESS FLINT, had two top five UK hits and the Gallagher and Lyle group which followed in the Seventies enjoyed wide success throughout Britain and America. It is as a song-writer, however, that Graham Lyle has continued to develop his international reputation. His songs have been recorded by a number of international artistes including PAUL SIMON and ART GARFUNKEL and BRYAN FERRY and he recently received the ultimate accolade, a US Grammy for his work with TINA TURNER.

'I was born in Bellshill in 1944 and my father was a draughtsman. We moved to Largs when I was two. My father was a musician of sorts. He played the lap Hawaiian guitar – a steel-string guitar, with metal slide. He didn't know anything musically . . . he'd just play the Hawaiian melodies instinctively, and I thought they were beautiful . . . he really had the touch. But when my friend and I learnt a few chords, within a week we knew more than my father did, musically. And, of course, now I play a lot of bottleneck and slide.

Anyway, this guitar was lying around the house and when rock'n'roll came out, I tried to play it, pulling the strings down. But they were so high – it was like bleeding fingers. So I gave that up for a while until my friend – Irvine Murray – got a guitar. We started on that plus a banjo that I bought when I was in the Scouts. We went through that whole thing, building our own guitars, getting import records from a little shop in Sauchiehall Street in Glasgow. It was a hardware shop which was run by this kind of Teddy Boy, and you went downstairs to a tiny stockroom. The guy was great . . . he was into the same things as us and would be importing, like, two albums of some things. We'd say, "Anything by . . . ?" – quite a range, actually, CHET ATKINS, early country, blues, CHUCK BERRY.

The first band used to practise up a close where I stayed! Great sound – acoustic guitars – and we wanted to play BUDDY HOLLY, although these things maybe only lasted a month. Then somebody would have an electric guitar or an amp and within a year there was a real band. This was called the RED VIKINGS or something, and it was hilarious for the other guitarist got it painted on his plectrums and his straps and everything. When we saw him the next week we said, "Look, we're sorry, we've changed our name to the BLUE FRETS." It was the Blue Frets for quite a long time, and I was the guitarist although I also played banjo and ukulele or whatever. Also drums, later.

I always had a good ear, I knew that right away. And I had the ability to pick up a melody, know whether things were in tune and so on. The band played at Scout dances, then we started running our own dances locally. We'd hire a hall . . . but it was Benny's (Gallagher) group in Saltcoats who were the real professionals. They had a van and played at gigs . . . the TULSANS . . . although Benny himself was also from Largs.

Then I stopped playing for, even at that time (1959 or 1960), I wanted to write songs. It was really the influence of BUDDY HOLLY and the EVERLY BROTHERS . . . the more melodic side of rock'n'roll always seemed to appeal more. I had also started a little studio of my own – a couple of tape recorders – and the Tulsans asked me to join them. I did a few gigs, then I'd take time off to write again.

At school, all I was interested in was music and art and, in Largs, I didn't get on with the music teacher. When I left Ardrossan Academy I worked in three or four jobs . . . in a graveyard (laughs), at IBM locally and so on. The band was run by a guy called Denis who had a café in Saltcoats, and the gigs were all over the Borders, Greenock, Edinburgh . . . the Tulsans also did Barrowlands, although I didn't play with them. And there was a little club at the top of West Nile Street (R&B Allnighter). Really good, small and packed, plus, of course, the Bobby Jones in Ayr, the miners' clubs . . . and they were trial by fire for any song that was your own. It had to be pretty strong or they stopped dancing . . . bad atmosphere. Everybody wanted to hear the Top Ten.

I was writing with Benny at this time and there was one gig, the American air base at Prestwick (where ELVIS touched down briefly) and there were these four black guys who would come up and sing with the band. By this time we were into early Tamla, and I was playin' drums. If the Americans got leave, they would come on the road with us and sing, and I know that the sound of their voices, the harmonies and the approach – the feel – influenced me. American music has always been my greatest influence. I never really liked the British end of things.

The BEATLES didn't impress us in the least, initially. In fact, our reaction . . . we had the same influences, early MIRACLES stuff, soul and R&B and I remember feeling quite resentful because we had never heard a band in Scotland playing the stuff we played, and we thought we were pretty good. We weren't so polished as

DEAN FORD AND THE GAYLORDS, but we had a good feel. Nearly all black American music.

We eventually made a couple of singles for Decca. We went down to audition at the same time as LULU – we all went down together, four or five bands, down on the Friday night, stayed in a hotel, did the audition at Decca studios then came home on the Saturday night! Dick Rowe, the guy who passed on the Beatles . . . poor bloke . . . had come up to Scotland, saw us at a gig in the Borders, and invited us down *(early 1964)*.

They were obviously keen on Lulu – she did *Shout* at the audition – and they took us although they weren't so sure. We were over the moon. The records were a couple of our own songs as A-sides – *Comes The Night,* a Bacharach-type ballad which really stretched us, augmented chords, and *With My Baby.* We also recorded a version of *La Bamba,* but it wasn't good. I think I was playin' drums with the band, but I played guitar on the record – a Burns – and the lead guitarist had a Gretsch. The group also had a lead singer, Drew Gault.

Not long after the session, Benny and I decided to give it a go in London. It meant chucking the band. We said let's all go down, and Drew came down for a while, but the others wouldn't go for it. So it was down to Benny and me. He was married by that time and I got married soon after moving to London *(1966).* We both had to have jobs, and I got one with a steel company as an export clerk. I had only been there a little while when my immediate boss went off to fight in the Seven Day War, and I got his job! I was selling thousands of tons of steel on the phone, taking orders, giving prices, and I hadn't a clue what I was doing. This was just before nationalisation.

We probably didn't write much at this time, because we were knackered! Workin' all day, and the only time we could write was when the kids had gone to sleep.

We were told by a friend that the BEATLES were opening a company – Apple – and he suggested we go along and play them a few songs. The guy, Terry Doran, liked them right away. He was a mate of the Beatles who had been a car salesman and road manager. He was an old rocker really, and the hippie thing was a bit confusing for him *(laughs)* but he was a lovely guy and in charge of Apple *(publishing)*! He said, "We're not exactly open yet, but we will be in the next two months and I want to sign you." We thought, we've heard that before but, right enough, two months later we got our first paid song-writing job.

They paid us £25 a week each which was more than we were getting in our jobs and it was terrific. We had to deliver product, though. I know everybody says

Apple was total chaos, but at the end of the week we had to come in and show them songs. It was great for us. PAUL McCARTNEY was working with MARY HOPKIN. He came in and said, "We need a B-side." There were six or seven teams of song-writers . . . the BADFINGER and GRAPEFRUIT guys . . . and McCartney said whoever writes the song for Mary will win a cake! And we won a cake! It was a song called *Sparrow* . . . extremely exciting times. And the PATHFINDERS were there, and I think they got the name "White Trash" from me. Tough band. Paul McCartney was genuinely concerned that the publishing side of Apple would develop. We got two or three B-sides and it was good for us.

Then McGUINNESS FLINT came along. They had been rehearsing for a year and they asked Benny to play bass. Benny says, "Okay, but I'm no' comin' if my friend's no' playin'" *(laughs)*. So I got hauled along and that first day we more or less wrote *When I'm Dead And Gone*. It was magic. It was a weird band – an avant-garde trombone player, Paul Rutherford, Denis Coulson singin' like Cocker, and Tom *(McGuiness)* and Hughie *Flint*. Hughie's a great player – rhythmically he's got it – and the band worked. I had an idea. I had never played mandolin in my life but I got a few chords out of it and we got into this groove. The melody was soon all there, and Benny came up with this idea for a lyric, about Robert Johnston.

I wasn't really a singer. I only ever sang harmonies with the TULSANS, but when we came to record it, I just sang it. THE BAND was a great influence on me at the time. I was absolutely knocked out by them. They used accordions, they were multi-instrumentalists, so we really tried to do that thing. Also the instruments were just lying around at Apple. For SERGEANT PEPPER, roadies had been told to go out and buy one of everything!

We got a number one with *When I'm Dead And Gone,* and then another hit, but tension developed within the band and it became uncreative. So, as a reaction to this, Benny and I decided to go out and play and sing ourselves. The writing suddenly had Scottish influences. We were still recording with Capitol, but A&M bought the contract and we were with them for ten years. Also, the sister company, Rondor, became our publishers.

GALLAGHER AND LYLE started really low key, in a transit van – clubs, then universities – touring all over. The first two albums were very acoustic, then *Seeds.* We had been listening to ethnic stuff which I had never really listened to before and RY COODER with that very echoey, atmospheric sound. We tried hard with a song about the Clearances, and that was the nearest we got to a Scottish blues.

We also tried singing in our natural accents, but I didn't like it. I didn't like the sound. I was too steeped in rock'n'roll and it didn't feel right to me. It was unnatural! I think the PROCLAIMERS are incredibly brave guys, for I think their style has limited entertainment value. We didn't want to be "folk" but Burns is my favourite poet, a strong influence, and I see it in the rhyming scheme of some of the songs I write now – for TINA TURNER. Also, rhythmically, there is something about Scottish and Irish musicians. Maybe a Celtic thing . . .

With *The Last Cowboy* LP, we toured with a large string section. It was rewarding creatively, but financially ruining. We had been building steadily but not selling a lot of albums or singles, and that was confining for me because I've always loved singles. But the style of music didn't lend itself to the Top Ten. Benny liked to play that *(acoustic)* style of music and we're talkin' about maybe doin' it again, but I'm too ambitious and the sort of music I want to write has got to have a broader canvas.

Musically, we didn't really change that much. We always had an interest in unusual chords and as our band was building up I was writing on electric guitar, which makes a difference. Also we had a good keyboard player *(Billy Livesey)* so we didn't have to support the whole song ourselves and things sounded good right away.

We worked very hard on the *Breakaway* album – *I Wanna Stay With You* . . . *Heart On My Sleeve* almost wrote itself . . . it was a natural, something which doesn't happen very often. Then ART GARFUNKEL heard a demo of *Breakaway* and, when we were recording the album, we got a phone call in the studio saying he was going to do it as a single. That was great, although we wanted to do it ourselves! Ours was a hit here, his was a hit in America, and few years later, he and PAUL SIMON did *A Heart In New York.*

That was one of the last songs Benny and I did together. As a band we did two more albums, one which was released and one which wasn't. We weren't gettin' on, we had been away from home for nine months of the year which meant difficult times for the families and, once, when I came home, my youngest son *(aged three)* didn't know who I was. It shocks you.

We kept on at it for a year and a half when things were not going well, but we weren't really writing together and I think that was the killer for, right from the early days, there was always a connection. I was gettin' particularly upset and couldn't deal with it. It was like a divorce.

The band was doin' pretty good and all the income except PRS went into one basket. We had a great team of guys, 100 per cent loyalty, a real family feeling, but we never got that US hit. We got very close with *I Wanna Stay With You,* and *Heart On My Sleeve* was a hit in Texas, and there were a few covers.

So I went solo in 1980/81 and started writing with everybody and anybody. I decided my only chance was to go for it as a writer, although I did a little recording in New York with Roy Halley who produced *Graceland* and engineered lots of Simon and Garfunkel's early stuff. I did a tribute to BOB MARLEY who meant a hell of a lot to me at that time. Once LENNON had died, Marley was my biggest influence and, musically, where THE BAND had stopped, to me Marley's band was where the groove went.

So I was writing sometimes three songs a day with different people – I just went crazy. Then I went over to Nashville and worked with Troy Seals, writing five songs and demoing them in ten days. Most of it was crap but it was getting something out of my system – What am I? What can I do? Coming out of it was Terry *(Brittan)*. I had had to work in the States with Art Garfunkel and, in Nashville, my things were getting more and more geared to America. And that's where my heart's always been.

I became much more interested in the lyric. Most of my involvement had been on the melody side and Troy Seals really taught me to take lyrics more seriously. Because, in Nashville, really it *is* lyrics. He had written with Will Jennings, and Dobie Gray did their demos. Stuart Hornall *(Rondor)* put us together, and it was an education. They are very professional there and Troy has this thing of how the song has to have an integrity. It has to have a starting point, a mental flow, a focus for the chorus. He didn't really say, "This is what happens", but just by working with the guy, you realise that a lyric is not just something that scans over and makes rough sense. He showed me a lot, and is another lovely guy. He introduced me to a lot of people in Nashville which is a lovely town – but unless you've got the key to the door . . . In America, song-writing is a respected profession, a craft. Over here, it's still, "It's alright for teenagers . . .", which is a bad thing. We have great ideas but I don't see people like me coming up as professional writers.

The first meeting I had with TERRY BRITTAN – he was a guy from Manchester who went to Australia as a young kid, played in bands and had a few hits, came back over here and started playing sessions. He joined the CLIFF RICHARD band, wrote *Devil Woman,* Cliff's only American hit, and he became involved with B. A. ROBERTSON, doing his backing tracks . . . nothing that would make me want to work with the guy. But that first day . . . it just happened.

A guy, a plugger at Chappell's called Paul Jenkins, put us together. We were both reluctant and were actually gonna pack it up that first day after a couple of hours because it wasn't working. I had been playing acoustic, and Terry said let's give it another go, try playing the electric guitar. We got a little groove going, plugged in the drum machine . . . and we were away. We got the melody with Terry singing any old thing, and put it on a cassette. Also, on the way to Terry's house I was listening to the radio and someone said on it "What's love got to do with it?", or something like that. Anyway, it registered. We were just singin' anything and when we got to the chorus I said, "Try singin' what's love got to do with it?" I knew it would scan, I didn't care about the notes, and the "Oh . . . oh" is almost the same as *When I'm Dead And Gone*! *(laughs)*.

Unless you've got a title that has a certain energy in it . . . what I find is that I view a phrase from a different angle – that's really what it's about, because everything's been said before. I then try to see the end point, and all the rest is using my craft. The first two lines are very important – they have to grab the attention – then the song has to take you on a little journey.

Anyway, the song was finished. We did the demo in a couple of days and put it into the publisher. We knew it was a great song and they came back within a couple of days saying, "There's four people want to record this song" – MANFRED MANN, BUCKS FIZZ, TINA TURNER and, maybe, CLIFF RICHARD or something. I can't remember. "What do you want to do?" Now four is really exceptional but Terry and I both went . . . "Tina Turner". They said, "What about Bucks Fizz? They sell a lot of records. Who's Tina Turner? No one gives a shit." We went . . . "No, we want Tina Turner to do it," and we're just so glad. You would not believe the difference it made to our professional lives. When it was going up the American charts, the phone used to ring every two minutes from America. These guys . . . Who's in the Top Ten? This one's good . . . we want him to write and produce. They don't give a shit who you are. That's the way they think. Do it again. Everybody, including QUINCY JONES, was saying, "Write something for us." It was the most amazing thing. We had to take the phone number off.

What's Love . . . is my most successful song. Winning the Grammy . . . I couldn't ask for more. But, on top of that, it was a wonderful thing to have Tina really come back with that song, and she says things to me like, "It has allowed me to *sing*." People used to say she's great on stage, what a rocker. Now they say, "Listen to Tina Turner *singing*."'

61

THE HEPCATS DOUG
MARTIN

DOUG MARTIN
DOUG MARTIN

62

CHAPTER SIX

DOUG MARTIN

Dundee and the East
'Have you seen Elvis Persley (sic)?'

Dundee can lay claim to a unique soul singing tradition – members of the AVERAGE WHITE BAND, BILLY MacKENZIE, MICHAEL MARRA, RICKY ROSS, GARY CLARKE, LORNA BANNON, MAFIA and the POOR SOULS. Doug Martin was the principal singer in the last two groups and is arguably the father of the family.

Andy Lothian had a problem. In Dundee, he believed he had found a group which could give an authentic challenge to the American soul sound which was beginning to sweep across Europe. But what to call them? As a former business associate of Brian Epstein, he knew that the name was all-important and it was keeping him awake. Suddenly his wife began talking in her sleep. 'Oh, the poor souls!' she exclaimed, obviously reflecting on those less fortunate than herself.

Doug Martin (b. 1941) came from a family of five boys and two girls and describes his early musical education as a case of 'hand-me-down harmonicas'. His father and two brothers played and when Doug or 'Doogie' or 'Dook' (as another harmonica player, Little Walter, was later to address him) acquired some proficiency on the instrument – around the age of seven – the family group began to play at concert parties which toured the public parks and local institutions.

A place he particularly remembers from that time is the 'Grubber' – a home for the elderly poor in Mollison Street – and one of the old worthies who befriended him was none other than 'Blin' Mattie', a blind lady accordionist who had been a familiar sight on the streets of Dundee in the earlier part of the century.

'I got a guitar back when there wasn't a single person who could tell you what to do with it. You sort of grabbed the frets and my father was a bookie's runner, so wi' a big family there wasn't the money for people to teach you. At secondary school *(Stobswell)* I asked to learn to play the trumpet, but the teacher said you had to be in the modified *(lowest)* class. In other words, you officially had to be daft to learn a musical instrument!

In the early Fifties the records were JO STAFFORD, TENNESSEE ERNIE FORD and novelty things like SPIKE JONES. I remember hearin' *Whole Lotta Shakin'* for the first time although you might have to sit by the radio for weeks before you'd hear it again. The only real chance o' hearin' the charts was if the family a' got bathed quick on a Sunday night and were in front o' the radio *(Luxembourg)* by 11 o'clock.

LONNIE DONEGAN was the first progression towards something that *you* could do. It was just a case o' tellin' a bunch a guys, maist o' whom didnae hae a clue aboot music – "You play this." Wi' me workin' in the big grocer's shop *(Dundee Eastern Co-operative Society, Strathmartine Road)*, I acquired a crackin' tea chest. I was a message boy wi' a difference. I biked everythin' but, on Tuesday an' Thursday afternoons an' Saturday mornin' I got the use o' a horse an' cart! Up the glens and it was tremendous. Along Riverside at that time there were dozens o' railway horses.

So we had the tea box *(double bass)* and it just so happened a guy – Eck MacKillop – had a guitar. Then oot came the washin' board and Ronnie Davie, who came from a musical family and was a puppeteer, he put a set o' dried milk tins thegither like drums, wi' sand in them to change the tones! An' somebody else rubbed wooden blocks wi' sandpaper! But even at that we tried to be professional. The tea box an' the washboard got a real good paint job, fae a guy who wis a sign-writer. The HEPCATS!

We were a skiffle group, but playin' LITTLE RICHARD, and the first thing we did wis ootside White's pub at the top o' Provost Road. On the pavement. Throwin' pennies in the hat an' runnin' when the polis came. Then we started to do the Black Watch clubs – Arthurstone Terrace, Bell Street, Strathmore Avenue, Rodd Road – sometimes three places in one night. The first 'proper' skiffle group was led by a guy called Terry Docherty – the KRAZY KATZ. He had big glasses like BUDDY HOLLY an' was doin' so well here, on the Palace Theatre, he went away to London.

> The Palace Theatre lay off Perth Road behind Queens Hotel and, as a variety theatre or vaudeville house, was still doing reasonable business in the Fifties. When trade began to tail off in the Sixties it made an attempt to cash in on the popularity of rock music with talent competitions and the occasional concert. On one such occasion, in 1964, Little Richard himself was due to open a British tour there, but was delayed at customs and failed to appear at the last minute.

In 1956, I met this guy who said his old man had made a guitar. His name was Harry Cole, a gem of a guy, and he said he would make one for me but there were certain things I had to pay for. My face fell. "A set o' machine heads, for example, would cost a pound, but the rest," he said, "I'll put in mysel'."

So it cost me a pound and I thought it went oot' o' tune, but nobody had told me you were supposed to renew your strings! Then I got a guitar for three quid, a boy got real drums and another pal got a Hofner Club 50 electric, which he let me play.

The first proper band was the MYSTERY MEN wi' Benny Esposito and when he left it became the HI-FOUR. We did the weekends at Methilhill Bowling Club in Leven and they had a 20 or 30-piece big band. It was the first good band I'd heard outside the Empress *(Ballroom, Dundee)* and the guitarist was Ron Moore who went to the ONE O'CLOCK GANG. The Hi-Four at this time was Eddie *(bass)*, Jimmy Smith *(guitar)*, me *(guitar)* – I was on an Eddie Cochran trip – and John Casey *(drums)*.

I also worked on the Dodgems at the Gussie Park Carnival. KAY STARR'S *Wheel Of Fortune* was the big hit, and *Rock Around The Clock*. Once there was a jivin' competition on the Dodgems' floor, wi' the music goin' above you. That was where you heard the hits by then – the Carni' – cos even when you were jivin' at, like, the Marryat Street Youth Club, there wisna' any rock'n'roll to jive to. It was a progression of bebop like *Mr Piano Player*. A load a crap.

Then, suddenly, a guy said to me, "Have you seen Elvis Persley *(sic)*?" It was pink suits an' yella jaickets then, and one day a guy I used to play wi' called Bud Rose (who was a SHADOWS fan) says, "I've found Cliff Richard!" This was Johnny Moran, who was a couple of years younger than me, and he looked great. The band became the JOHNNY HUDSON HI-FOUR and we began to work all over Scotland for Andy Lothian. Sometimes we would back singers like VINCE EAGER and once, PAUL RAVEN – who became GARY GLITTER – took pleurisy and my mother nursed him in Fleming Gardens.'

JOHNNY HUDSON
(photocopy)
ALBERT BONICI

Andy Lothian was the son of a Dundee bandleader of the same name, who owned one of the city's premier dance halls, the Palais, in South Tay Street. Himself a musician, he first made his name with the Sunday night *Top Ten Club* which had begun in 1955 at a time when the Public Entertainment Act precluded dancing on a Sunday.

'You weren't even allowed to stand still! Bouncers moved you on an' you'd say to lassies – are you goin' roond? Everybody walked round and round and at ten when it finished, the whole charade walked out the door and down to the coffee stall at the foot of the Overgate! Wi' the Teddy Boy suits, they called it the Monkey Parade.'

By 1960 the club was highly successful and Lothian was beginning to spread his promotional and managerial wings. A business associate named John Marshall ran a club in Cologne and it was to there – the Storeyville Jazz Club on the

Kaiser Wilhelmsring – that Andy sent the Hudson Hi-Four. Not only were they the first Dundee rock group to work abroad, the BEATLES themselves had only just arrived in Hamburg. The experience proved important for both groups.

'We were told to pick up this tall guy wi' fair hair at Victoria Station, an' it was LONG JOHN BALDRY. He was a folk/blues singer and this was his first taste of rock'n'roll. The club had been a jazz club and at first it was a bit of a struggle, but there was a terrific black band – WILLIE WILSON AND THE DOWNBEATS – with fantastic gear like Fenders when we had Vox 15s, and we learned all these great, new American songs.'

When the group returned to Dundee they were 'tough' in the same way that the Beatles had hardened their sound and repertoire. One of the first to appreciate the fact was a 13-year-old boy who attended Dundee High School, Donnie Coutts, who at that time lived in Thompson Street in Dundee's West End.

WILLIE WILSON
Godfather of Dundee
Soul DOUG MARTIN

DONNIE COUTTS

DONNIE COUTTS: 'I had been to see folk like PAUL ANKA and EDDIE COCHRAN at the Caird Hall and had been playing drums in a school band *(the Spotlights)* for a couple of years. One night in 1960 I went to Robie's *(the West End Palais)* off Hawkhill to see a marathon twisting competition. The band was the STACCATO FIVE with Drew Larg singin' and to me it was fantastic. Rock'n'roll and chart stuff. They played alternately with records and Andy Lothian was the announcer. He said, "Come back tomorrow, we hope Cathie (Connolly, the champion twister, who was in a state of collapse but about to enter *The Guinness Book of Records*) will still be twisting!" So I went along the next night and was disappointed because it wasn't the same band. But when the HI-FOUR started . . . this was *it*! They were doing the soul stuff they had learned in Germany – CHUCK JACKSON, BOBBY BLAND and JERRY BUTLER – so since I worked at Low's Record Shop on a Saturday, I began looking out records. I discovered that Motown was released on Oriole – the CONTOURS, BARRET STRONG, then the IMPRESSIONS – and I started passing the material on to Johnny Hudson to learn.'

THE HI-FOUR
DOUG MARTIN

DOUG MARTIN: 'This wee laddie in his High School uniform . . . and when we started tourin', the reaction was fantastic. In Shetland it was maybe the first group they'd ever seen live . . . Orkney, Kyle of Lochalsh once, plus the North-east for Bert Ewen and Albert Bonici, the Borders for Duncan MacKinnon and Barry Riddle, and Mary Yardley booked us for Glasgow and Balloch. Then Arran was on the go. One Saturday night we travelled from Wick to Ayrshire for the paper boat to Arran . . . a wee, open boat, so we could make the Sunday night show. But the Glasgow folk went to Arran and this gave us a following at places like Woodend Jazz Club in Jordanhill and the Carioca in Bearsden. Plus we were still backin' these would-be stars.

Then we went to Hamburg *(1963)*. The BEATLES had made it by that time and we played wi' TONY SHERIDAN, the BOBBY PATRICK BIG SIX and ALEX HARVEY. Once Alex's band was makin' a record so we had to do a 12-hour shift ourselves! The boss kept comin' up wi' these Top Ten specials *(drinks)* an' at the end you needed a scraper to get us aff the flair!

The first time I saw Alex was in 1956 in Dundee. He had won this competition to find Scotland's Tommy Steele and he was in the Caledonian Tailor's in the Wellgate, signin' photies if you bought a rock'n'roll suit! The BIG SOUL BAND was his best group. Good, raw soul. I used to stand in as rhythm guitar.

The day we arrived back in Dundee, Lothian told us we were playin' wi' the Beatles at the Caird Hall *(September 1963)*. JOHN LENNON was the big man and I went up to him and mentioned some guy who had been showin' us photographs of himself and Lennon in Hamburg. "How am I supposed to remember everybody I've met?" says Lennon and I was shattered. RINGO rescued me though. He comes over, offers this handful of jewellery *(handshake)* and we chatted about the club in Hamburg.'

The HI-FOUR became the POOR SOULS in 1964 with Chick Taylor playing guitar, Dougie playing bass, Hudson, rhythm, and Casey drums, and around this time they were at the height of their powers. They spent a year in England and released one excellent single for Decca – the Lesley Duncan song, *When My Baby Cries* – but despite fairly wide public acclaim, the hit record eluded them.

DOUG MARTIN: 'At one point, I was offered solo, soul-type promotion, but I'd had enough. I just felt like goin' away an' bein' normal. So I worked in Arran in the summers and was a normal Glasgow bus driver during the winter months.'

THE POOR SOULS
FABULOUS MAGAZINE

The baton passed to Donnie Coutts. He was already a central figure in the Dundee music scene in the mid-Sixties and a keen observer of what was happening.

DONNIE COUTTS: 'In the absence of the Poor Souls, the top groups around Dundee were the HONOURS *(whose guitarist Jim Kelly was later to join the group HONEYBUS)* and a couple of groups from Montrose, TOMMY DENE AND THE TREMORS *(guitarist, Billy Bremner, later of ROCKPILE)* and the BLACK HAWKS. I was in a group called the WISE BROTHERS and later the SYNDICATE *(into which he introduced a keyboard player, Mike Fraser)*.

We worked for Andy Rettie who managed a Perth group called the VIKINGS. Their guitarist was a guy called Dougie Wightman, and their bass player, ALAN GORRIE.'

Gorrie was to become an art student in Dundee where he made a number of musical connections important to his subsequent career, and when the Vikings experienced personnel problems, it was first to Fraser and then to Coutts that he turned (1965/66). The group auditioned (unsuccessfully) for EMI at Abbey Road and, back in Scotland, the 'veteran', Drew Larg was drafted in as vocalist. They carried on playing the Scottish circuit and, with the pirate radio station – Radio Scotland – gaining popularity, recorded a single for Andy Lothian's ALP record label. It was a little-known PAUL SIMON song called *Bad News Feeling* and entered the radio station chart at number nine.

DONNIE COUTTS: 'We complained and they put it up to number four *(Doug Martin wrote the B-side)*. We got a chance to go to the Locomotive club in Paris for two weeks, but you needed a parent to sign your passport if you were under 21, and my father wouldn't sign. He was upset that I'd given up my job and virtually ignored me for a time. We signed up with Peter Walsh at Starlight for 10 per cent commission but we were living from hand to mouth because we didn't know you could sign on the broo! We stayed in the Madison Hotel where all the groups stayed and people like DAVID BOWIE, MAN, AMEN CORNER and the FIFTH COLUMN *(Gerry Rafferty and Joe Egan)* were all there at that time.

Then we got a flat at Finsbury Park and again there were loads of groups – the SCOTS OF ST JAMES, the SENATE, and the WILD FLOWERS from Newcastle. This was Paul Rogers' group.

We were doing gigs all over England but it was crippling us. Walsh then asked if we would like to become a 15 per cent group *(ie pay 15 per cent commission)* and he would get us better work. We needed the money the agency owed us to get home, though, and after that things went from bad to worse. Alan was fixing himself up with the Scots of St James and Dougie Wightman had fallen out with Drew so, when we were up playing at Dundee Art School, I filled up an application to do Town Planning.'

> He subsequently pursued this career before departing the professional scene, although Coutts was to make an important musical connection. While in Dundee, he had given great encouragement to a young drummer named Robbie McIntosh and, on his return for his college interview, he promised the Senate (now, essentially, a grouping of Glasgow musicians in London) that he would mention their drumming vacancy to his Dundee protégé.

DONNIE COUTTS: 'I came up in the plane with Drew. We had missed the Shuttle and a Dundee roadie, George Ward, waited all night for us. We went to see Robbie and you just had to ask him once. Drew and I stayed in Dundee and Robbie and Mike went back down.'

MIKE FRASER

Mike Fraser was the brother of a well-respected Scottish jazz pianist, Kenny Fraser, and by the late Sixties was himself an accomplished keyboard player.

MIKE FRASER: 'I took a clerical job for six weeks then the organist with the SENATE, Brian Johnston *(formerly Golden Eagles)* left. I was asked to join and teamed up with Robbie and Alex Lidgerwood *(vocals/guitar)*. We went to Germany with DUANE EDDY, BEN E. KING, BIG MAYBELLE, then, back in London, we were asked to do a club in Rome. We were in Frankfurt in December 1967 and drove straight there. The band went well but the van was stolen and we were cleaned out. We only lasted three months after that. A Dundee guitarist, Jim McAra, joined briefly, but to no avail.

I got a job with an English group called MAL AND THE PRIMITIVES. The singer was big in Italy and the drummer was Pick Withers *(later with DIRE STRAITS)*. Soon Robbie had joined, then Alex, and we got an apartment. It was a great time. Robbie then went to a good French group, the PIRANHAS, and was spotted by Brian Auger. He went back to London and teamed up *(later)* with Jim Mullen and Alex again. I was also briefly in London, but preferred Italy and when I went back, I began to get loads of session work.'

> Fraser worked at the top of his profession in Italy, latterly with ENNIO MORRICONE, and others. In London Robbie once more made contact with ALAN GORRIE who was by then in a country/rock group named FOREVER MORE – their guitarist in the late Sixties was Glasgow-born OWEN MacINTYRE. Gorrie's art college colleagues, Molly Duncan and Roger Ball, were by then in demand as a session horn section, the DUNDEE HORNS, and playing with the group MOGUL THRASH. They began to organise informal demos to record some soul-based material and, by the summer of 1971, a group was taking shape. 'I was working in London and, by chance, met Donnie Coutts who was heading for Gorrie's flat in West Kensington. It was the type of musician's flat with which I was later to become very familiar – not much furniture, but a nice tape machine – and the music was instrumental and more funky than the current soul sounds. I asked who he was listening to and was not much the wiser when the name QUINCY JONES was offered.
>
> "And will you sing yourself?" I inquired. "Yes," said Alan, "and there's going to be another guy singing as well. His name's Hamish Stuart."

Dougie Martin, Donnie Coutts and Mike Fraser are all performing in the Dundee area at the time of writing, although only Fraser retains music as a full-time occupation.

Martin and Coutts had a marvellous reprise in the late Seventies/early Eighties with a six-piece Dundee soul group named MAFIA.

THE VIKINGS Back: l to r Doug Wightman, Drew Larg, Alan Gorrie. Front: Mike Fraser, Donnie Coutts
DOUG MARTIN

CHAPTER SEVEN

ALAN GORRIE

'It has to be a struggle'

I had come into contact with Alan Gorrie during his Dundee years and my group the HALOS had occasionally supported the VIKINGS at local dances. In the summer of 1966 my friend Alastair Swanson and I went for a fortnight's holiday to London. We were between school and university and the world was our proverbial whelk. We stayed in an extremely crummy hotel in Porchester Square, Paddington but this was bearable (geddit?) because the purpose of our visit was to gross out on music and this we duly did: HORACE SILVER at Ronnie Scott's old club in Gerard Street; the NEW YARDBIRDS with Page and Beck; the IKE AND TINA TURNER REVUE; the ROLLING STONES (six bob); JESS RODEN (Alan Bown Set); IAN GILLAN (Episode Six); and – OTIS REDDING – in a club, 20 feet away!

We returned to Dundee with an armful of records and for my group's last performance we were able to give them not only obscure Otis Redding, but Sam and Dave among others.

At the same venue four days later, the Vikings appeared. Alan Gorrie, wearing Roger McGuinn sunglasses says, 'We'll start with a song by Sam and Dave.' As they say in Dundee . . . 'It'd mak ye seek.'

'I was born and brought up in Perth, and stayed there until I was 18. My father was a bandleader, a really good piano player whose main interest was jazz. But he didn't teach me to play – you can't teach your own kid to play – and anyway, all I wanted to do at that time was play guitar. I liked ELVIS, but I think *Love Me Tender* turned me off.

The first band, at school, was the FALCONS *(1961)* and in about two years, that had turned into the VIKINGS – Dougie Wightman, myself, Roy Fleming and Graham Duncan. We played R&B, DRIFTERS, COASTERS. I went to college in 1964 and it was in my first year that Graham Duncan left, and Donnie Coutts and Mike Fraser joined. I was doing a General Course at Dundee Art College, but I wasn't cut out for it.

There was no Perth scene – some good musicians and bands like the CYCLONES and the ERLE BLUE STARS who became GARY AND THE HIGHLANDERS – but they played pure pop and never influenced anything. The Vikings were as good as anybody in Scotland except the POOR SOULS, whom no one could touch. Our manager was Andy Rettie, and he got us gigs all over Scotland until 1965, when we threw in our lot with Andy Lothian.

Dundee, to me, was soul music and Dougie Martin was a major influence on how I sing, or what I think a singer should be. STEVE WINWOOD and Dougie were the only two British singers who, for my money, were worth tuppence. I thought the Poor Souls name, though, was too self-effacing, and England paid no attention to Scotland at that time, anyway.

The prevalence of soul music was only East Coast. The Glasgow bands – with the exception of the BIG SOUL BAND and maybe the BIG SIX, whom I didn't hear – did not have a vocalist who could approach Dougie Martin and didn't work on the vocals to the same extent. Their soul music, therefore, was not as intact as in Dundee, where the emphasis was on vocals. If you couldn't sing, you couldn't make it – and I'm not biased, because I don't belong to Dundee – but it was Dundee that influenced me, and it was quite similar to the Liverpool scene in many ways.

It was in Perth, however, that the idea for the AVERAGE WHITE BAND first took root. The Vikings were resident at the Falkirk La Bamba club, and I helped set up a similar place in Perth called the Blue Workshop. These places made me see there was a thing for R&B in Scotland. I had met ROGER BALL and MOLLY DUNCAN at Dundee Art College, and I asked them to come to the Blue Workshop where they played with Glasgow jazzmen JIM MULLEN, ANDY PARK and BOBBY WISHART. MIKE FRASER and I would also sit in, and even ROBBIE MacINTOSH *(who was only 15)* and I think there was a tacit understanding that someday there was gonna be an awful band coming out of this. This was between 1964 and 1966, and the VIKINGS went to London at the end of this period.

Our first venture in London was very short-lived, because it was a struggle – it has to be a struggle – and one or two people couldn't take it. I didn't go back because I'd nothing to go back to. I joined the SCOTS OF ST JAMES, a Glasgow/Stirling band, and ONNIE MacINTYRE was in that band. They weren't as good as the band I'd come out of, but it was a way of staying in London with people who talked the same language, and they had the prospect of some gigs abroad. So we went to Germany – the Storeyville Clubs in Frankfurt and Cologne – and we did an American nuclear base in Kassel *(1967)*. We were popular with the black guys at the base and that was my first twig that I could do something in America. We also realised that the singer – JIMMY OAKLEY – couldn't cut it, so when we came back to Glasgow, we picked up HAMISH STUART. I had seen him once at La Bamba with DREAM POLICE, and was impressed. Later, he went back to that group, and took them to London.

Over the next three years, a lot happened. SCOTS OF ST JAMES became FOREVER MORE with MICKY TRAVIS, and had blues and folk influences, although not Scottish – Scottish music to me meant country dance, and never really appealed; Molly and

74

Roger graduated as architects, came to London and ended up in a group called
MOGUL THRASH; and Robbie was in Europe, first with the SENATE, then BRIAN AUGER.
Scottish groups, however, were nowhere at this time. Apart from STONE THE CROWS
who became an influential band – MAGGIE BELL and JIMMY DEWAR were great singers
– there was only MARMALADE, who were like the Scottish Tremeloes, although
Dean was technically a great singer. Stone the Crows were going somewhere until
Les Harvey died, and Roger and Molly had played with them.

I was out of work for a year *(1970)* and signing on. I was offered the gig with
FAMILY – which would have made me some money – and Mike *(Fraser)* wanted me
to go to Italy, but I turned them down. I wanted to go west, and I wanted to put the
band together that was in my mind.

By 1971, Robbie had left Brian Auger and we had found a manager, Robin
Turner, who was with Island Records and had some financial backing. Muff
Winwood, though, said, "It's hard for an instrumental band to get a hit," – even
although Hamish and myself were both singing! So Island wouldn't sign us. Of
course, the band itself was a bit uncertain of Hamish at first. He's a shy bloke and
had come from this really awful BERSERK CROCODILES thing, where he had picked up
some bad vocal habits. He and Robbie became friendly, however, and that was
things set.

We did an album for MCA *(Show Your Hand, 1972)* but they were doing us no
favours in America. Our first trip there had been to do BONNIE BRAMLETT's album
(she of Delaney and Bonnie) and it was a great experience. We learned so much. We
met SLY STONE and BOBBY WOMACK who were raving about the band, and we learned
recording techniques. Also, Bruce MacAskill, who had been all over as Eric
Clapton's personal manager, became our manager.

We did some more demos for MCA, but they weren't interested and we didn't
want to go back to Britain, for we had peaked as a cult band. One night, we heard
that JERRY WEXLER *(Atlantic Records)* was in LA, and staying at Alan Pariser's, who
managed Delaney and Bonnie. Wexler heard our stuff and signed it the next day.
Atlantic was where we wanted to be, and Jerry took the tapes to ARIF MARDIN, whom
he thought should produce us.

The first sessions *(for The White Album)* were amazing. We went to Miami and
ARETHA FRANKLIN was just finishing her stuff with all her great musicians – it was
mind-blowing! How could we follow that? But we had to, and both Wexler and
Mardin made a number of useful suggestions. Great ears, and Tommy Dowd was
the same. They knew how to put the jigsaw together better than we did. It was the
post-diploma school!

AVERAGE WHITE BAND ALAN GORRIE

Then we came up to New York to improve the drum sound – Arif thought it was too soft for a monster like Robbie, and felt we should use Gene Paul. We ended up doing most of the album at Atlantic Studios in New York, and that was just a phenomenal two weeks. We then headed back to Scotland, while Arif mixed the album.

In the August of 1973, we did the New York Bottom Line and the Troubadour in Los Angeles, and it was the happiest musical time of our lives. The stars were turning out, we had arrived, and that week at the Troubadour was the epitome of everything I'd ever wanted to do. Nothing could touch us. *(Unfortunately, something did touch them – death.)* Robbie had actually predicted his own demise. He used to say things like, "I'll never see thirty," or "Somebody is going to have to die in this group before it gets attention."

The night in question wasn't as bizarre as it has been made to sound. A perfectly happy situation apart from one crazy character who spiked everybody. I survived, Robbie didn't. We were all so exhausted after the Troubadour week. Two or three shows a day, burned out, no resistance. On a different day Robbie would have been sick and taken to hospital. But his metabolism was low. Also he was a heavy drinker, but never a dope fiend. None of us were. We liked the hard-drinking

76

ALAN GORRIE
ALAN GORRIE

Scottish image.

The record did nothing to begin with, and it was disappointing, but our lives were in disarray. By November/December, it began to pick up. Steve Ferrone came in, and Arif said, "You have to get back on the horse," and we went back into the studio. In retrospect, they should have released more singles from what was a classic album. Apart from the title track, I didn't like *Cut The Cake* much.

The Average White Band was really the two years with Robbie and the shine had come off things, although the next while was amazing. We were the first white act to have a number one single and album in both the pop and R&B charts in the same week, and the black community became our staunchest fans in the States. In fact, they still are. Last year we went out with the re-vamped AWB, just as an occasional thing, and there were a lot of young and middle-aged black people really enjoying it.

The first band, however, began to grow away from common musical influences. I may have been the titular leader, but Robbie was the driver. His taste in music was impeccable and he would keep us all in line. He was the musical heart, an ingénu, and the funniest person I'd ever met. A one-off. *Feel No Fret* was a good album, and even Hamish would agree we had a great time making it. It had a cohesiveness, but later there was needle. It happens to every band, of course, and the band had begun to outlive its usefulness to world music. We had one more hit – *Let's Go Round Again* – our Philadelphia song and our swan song.

The band's name came from my wife Jean. A Montrose fellow called Rab Wyper who was friendly with us, worked at the Foreign Office and used to speak jokingly about places which were too hot for 'the average white man'. We were looking for a name and Jean said, "What about the Average White Band?" I think it was quite a brave name, and it was a winner.

I did a solo album for A&M next but it wasn't released in the UK. Hamish had the same experience. The company changed personnel and we went out with the bathwater. I've also done some production – UK PLAYERS, JEFFREY WILLIAMS and some others, and I write for other people. You can't stop doing music, wakening up with a tune in your head, although now I have a better overview. Scotland has had a lot of attention in the States in recent years . . . DANNY WILSON had a great single. I'm very attracted to Scotland again.'

ROBBIE MACINTOSH
(Author's footnote)

Robbie MacIntosh was born in Dundee in 1950 and, unusually for a Dundonian, was the son of a film star. The American actor Bonar Colleano who, like Ronald Reagan, was famous for his post-war B-movies, spent some time filming at Barry Buddon Army Camp near Dundee and, following a brief liaison with Robbie's mother, left something more than memories behind.

I was in a school band which used to perform at youth club dances in Broughty Ferry. One time, our drummer, Bill Findlay, was unavailable and my good friend DONNIE COUTTS, who had his finger on the musical pulse then and still does, recommended this young lad. 'He's only 15,' said Donnie, 'but he's brilliant.'

Robbie's home at this time was in Kincardine Street, off Dundee's Hawkhill. My own father had lived there when he was young and it was a poor place then, but even I was not prepared for what was coming. The flat appeared to have no furniture or carpets until Robbie – a tall, skinny boy with curly hair – led us into his bedroom. Against a wall stood crude bunk-beds, again with minimal covering, but beside the window was a gleaming Ludwig drum kit.

'Whar did ye get that?' asked Johnnie Lynch, whose van we were using.

'Ma auntie bought it,' replied Robbie, and I later discovered that Robbie's auntie was a very important person in his life.

'An' 'iv ye no' got cases?' asked Johnnie, as Robbie began to move the drums.

'Nup.'

We trooped down the stairs not saying very much, but I knew what was on everyone's mind. Only RINGO STARR and KEITH MOON had Ludwig drum kits.

We drove to Broughty Ferry and when we met the rest of the band, their reaction was the same – 'What is this?' I respected Donnie's judgment so there was no question of an audition, but I thought it wise to have a quiet word with the youngster. I, after all, was almost 17.

'We're gonna start wi' *Can't Explain*,' I said, thinking of something strong but simple from THE WHO. 'Just take it easy until you get the feel.'

'Gie's the tambourine,' replied Robbie, and again we watched open-mouthed as he attached it to the top of his hi-hat. What *was* this? The curtains would be opened at 7.30 and, approximately six seconds later, all our questions were answered. The opening chords rang out, there was Robbie absolutely powering his way in, with an offbeat fill that had us raising our eyebrows.

'I gotta feelin' inside . . .' I certainly did.

'He's more of a jazz drummer,' said one of the band at the interval.

The next time I saw Robbie, he had the air of a man about him. He had left school, his hair was longer and on his arm was a girl from the local fee-paying school. He also, apparently, still had the flat and was gigging with some of the best local musicians at a residency in Newport. This would have been around 1967 and, the following year, he joined an established soul group originally from Glasgow called the SENATE. Mike Fraser was the piano player and Alex Lidgerwood the guitarist/singer. They were absolutely dynamite and played at Dundee University on one memorable Saturday night when JON HENDRICKS was appearing earlier in the evening at the University Jazz Club. This was a perfect day.

Robbie and Mike next went to Italy with the Senate and from there to London. Robbie joined Brian Auger's OBLIVION EXPRESS with Jim Mullen as guitarist, and really, a musician could not do better than have the respect of such outstanding players.

Tam Parks, the renowned Dundee drummer and roadie, has a few good stories from this time. In London, Robbie married Edith and she gave birth to a son, Brandon.

TAM PARKS
DAVY BOY

'One night,' says Tam, 'Robbie an' me are ha'en a drink, when there's a knock at the door.'

'See wha that is,' says Robbie, planking the half bottle of gin.

'So, eh go doon the stair an' open the door. It's Stevie Marriot.'

'Are you Robbie?' asks Marriot in the anticipated cockney voice.

'Na, eh'm Tam . . . 'mon up the stair.'

Stevie Marriot, at this time a big star, goes up to the room. Robbie, without a second thought and as if he's known the Small Face all his life, says, 'Well, Stevie: Will ye hae a gin?'

'Nice one, Robbie,' says Marriot, 'only, would you like to play on my solo album?'

Again, without a moment's hesitation, Robbie turns to his wife . . .

'Edith, put the bairn doon the stair, we'll go and dae Stevie's session . . .'

'One night *(Tam again)* we're in Tramps disco and QUEEN are about to break.

'Look out,' says a trendy punter, 'here comes Freddie . . . 'e's a star now.' Everyone studiously ignores Freddie Mercury, except Robbie.

'Ho!' he calls, gesticulating for the singer to come over. Robbie is very drunk.

'Dinna bather aboot them,' he says, 'they're jist jealous. Eh think yir bra. Eh watch ye every week.'

'Sorry?' says Mercury, 'I'm sorry, what do you mean, you watch me every week?'

Robbie tries to sit up straight on the stool, and focus.

'*The Freddie Starr Show*,' he finally says, bemused. 'Eh watch it every week.'

There are lots of stories like that about the man who may have been the first member of the White Band to attract the attention of Atlantic Records, and who was subsequently offered the LITTLE FEAT job, only to turn it down in favour of his countrymen. His faith proved justified.

Robbie MacIntosh died in 1973 after being given poisonous chemicals at a celebration party for the Average White Band, who were soon to go to number one in the American charts. Although *never* a hard drugs man, he was an experienced drinker and it was his confused refusal to be sick that killed him.

ROBBIE MACINTOSH August 1973
"WELCOME TO LA"
MacCARNEGIE

CHAPTER EIGHT

RAB NOAKES

'The hem of Little Richard's garment'

RAB NOAKES, like MAE McKENNA and JOHN MARTYN who are interviewed later, came to electric music via the Scottish folk scene. Like GERRY RAFFERTY, with whom he later teamed up in the group STEALERS WHEEL, he attracted a fair bit of attention in London in the late Sixties and made a number of quality albums although he failed to make a commercial breakthrough. He subsequently worked in radio and is now a Senior Producer with Radio Scotland.

'My mother comes from Dundee but the Noakes name comes originally from Kent. My great-grandfather was a journeyman joiner on the *Mars* training ship – a ship berthed in the Tay for orphans and delinquents – then later he was apparently a timekeeper on both Tay rail bridges. I was born in St Andrews in 1947. The first couple of years were spent in Newport then my father went to work in the Post Office in Cupar, so we moved there.

My mother used to sing during the war with a couple of big bands and broadcast from the BBC in Glasgow at one stage. But of course it has always been hard for women in this business for a number of reasons. She would have sung the pop songs of the day plus a Scottish repertoire, like *Rowan Tree*.

I was growing up in the early Fifties and I always remember KEITH RICHARDS saying later that he remembered what the world was like before rock'n'roll. To some extent I do too and it was far from dull. Some lovely songs, although some were daft and voices were up front. I remember *On Top Of Old Smokey* and kitsch Scottish stuff from Robert Wilson. Exposure to music came in some odd ways: like guisers comin' round . . . young teenagers at Hallowe'en singin' pop songs, and I was fascinated. I can clearly remember a boy and girl comin' in and singin' *Buttons And Bows*.

I started to sing then . . . I obviously had an ear and I went to a Miss Neilson's singin' class when I was six. I loved these people of that initiative and boldness and *Westering Home* was my first public performance. My mother told me to keep an eye on something in the room, so I wouldn't be distracted.

Rock'n'roll happened when I was eight or nine. We had an accumulator radio whose battery had to get filled up every so often, and then we moved from rented accommodation to a brand new council house. There were all these families with

Opposite: RAB NOAKES R. NOAKES

older kids who then began to influence me. Some of the homes had radiograms and a great deal of my musical education was sittin' on the kerb outside listening to other people's record collections. ELVIS was the main one, BUDDY HOLLY, EDDIE COCHRAN . . . and skiffle came about then. *Last Train To San Fernando* and the carnivals. We had an open bit of ground called the Fluthers where the carnivals came after they had left the Links Market in Kirkcaldy or the Lammas Market in St Andrews. That was fantastic . . . then the cafés . . . and I would buy the magazines that had lyric sheets.

The local record shop was *(and still is)* J A Stewart's in Cupar and one outstanding memory was seeing a poster of Elvis and hearing *All Shook Up* inside. If there was ever an event that pointed me in another direction it was that. I wanted to look like that, sound like that, be that . . . and my grandad took us to see *Loving You*.

I picked up a guitar first around 1960/61. I always thought it beyond me because there was no one there to show you how to play. I also wanted a piano and eventually went to violin classes which was useful, especially for left hand vibrato and so forth. But I continued to sing with wee groups and learn songs which I would sing at Christmas parties . . . *Mary's Boy Child,* and that was my first inkling of how to perform and have an effect on people. I thought, "This is no' bad!"

I didn't really meet any bands until I was 15 or so. There was a guy who had been in the Merchant Navy and he encouraged me. I suppose I was a good mimic and that's how you learn how to phrase and so forth. We'd go to the Drill Hall in Cupar every Saturday and watch VINCE NEWMAN AND THE VELTONES knockin' out the hits. They were fae Leven and hot at the time. I was extremely enthusiastic.

Academically, though, things were going downhill from getting a reasonable pass in the qually *(11-Plus).* The classes were overloaded and I could never get a grip of mathematics. I had been put in a classical stream and the whole thing just was all wrong. I couldna' get a hold o' anythin'.

So, my old man comes up with this idea for me to join the Civil Service as a clerical officer. I didna' really fancy the job much but the places people wanted staff were Glasgow and Edinburgh and I came to Glasgow in 1963. It was an interesting experience coming to the city and the first time I walked up Union Street, I saw an advert for a package tour that was coming to the Odeon. The EVERLYS, whom I loved, were headlining with Micky Most as compère, the ROLLING STONES, BO DIDDLEY . . . and LITTLE RICHARD, who closed the first half. I have never before or since seen anything like him. I had bought a good seat in Row D and he came off the stage at one point, up one side round the back and down the other. Then he started takin' his claes aff and the shirt landed right in front o' me! I dived right into the mêlée and for years in my drawer I had the cuff of Little Richard's shirt.

I stayed in Glasgow for a year and a half and I went to every package tour that came. The only lot I missed were the BEATLES, and most of the tours had good Americans like CARL PERKINS, CHUCK BERRY, JERRY LEE LEWIS, quite often backed by the NASHVILLE TEENS. It was the time of the mods which was gang-orientated, although great fashion. The BEATSTALKERS, PATHFINDERS and POETS were big then . . . ALEX HARVEY was somebody you heard about and we went to clubs like the Cucaracha in Dundas Street and Klooks Kleek in Sauchiehall Street.

Also I'd been hearing the name of BOB DYLAN from the BEATLES and the ANIMALS and he just blew me sideways. I got my mother and father to give me a guitar for Christmas that year *(1964)* and I just sat and beavered away. The first song I managed to play was *The Ballad Of Hollis Brown* and within six months I could do clawhammer and picking. So the next time I was in Cupar at the Royal Hotel Folk Club I jumped up and played a couple of songs. Davie Craig *(later of HIGH SPEED GRASS)* and Willie Gillespie were there and we hooked up as friends after that. Davie had a WOODY GUTHRIE album and one of his neighbours in Dairsie had LEADBELLY records, so this guy (Mike Field) became a font of knowledge, and the progress was quite good then. We went as a group to folk song clubs and I left Glasgow to work in Alloa which was a bright wee town at the time. So with my girlfriend I began to go to folk clubs virtually every night of the week. That was a two-way process whereby you could play your own songs and listen to others – locals, guests and sometimes the older singers like JIMMY MacBEATH and JEANNIE ROBERTSON.

We went to London in 1966 and I worked with the Social Security. It meant I saw the blossoming of the INCREDIBLE STRING BAND but the big thing for me was BERT JANSCH. It was hard to believe he was Scottish but I was attracted to it and I was now hearing all types of music. I was most interested in the guitar players and BOB DYLAN. In fact, I'm still fascinated by him.

We did the rounds of the good folk clubs but, financially, it was a struggle and I came back to Scotland in May 1967. I worked as a gardener for Fife County Council and you could just wander behind this lawn-mower, thinking freely! Then I worked at the sugar beet in Cupar but things became uncomfortable at home so I moved back to Glasgow and Robin McKidd *(also HIGH SPEED GRASS)* came through with me. He introduced me to a lot of old-time country stuff . . . CLARENCE ASHLEY and DOC WATSON . . . and you'd suddenly see connections. Scottish folk music, Appalachian music, the EVERLYS . . . it seemed to have some consistency.

So Robin and I played at the Folk Centre in Montrose Street *(Glasgow)* and met people like BILLY CONNOLLY and JOHN MARTYN. Billy and TAM HARVEY were doing something musically similar to us, and Robin and Billy would swap odd bits and pieces. We then went south again and had quite a tight act . . . bluegrass, the old timers, and I would do a solo thing. I was beginning to write, and between us we could put two good half-hours together. We did a tour of East Anglia for Brian Bird and went down a storm so we were confident going into London but, of course, nothing happened. We wound up doing a residency at the King Lud, Ludgate Circus, five nights a week, and performing bits of everything. That tightened things up, but McKidd split and I drifted back to Fife and then Davie Craig and I got a job in Denmark.

By the time I came back, Arthur Argo was gettin' me work and I had also met GERRY RAFFERTY who was soon to be playin' with Billy. We had met at Billy's house in White Street and everybody sang what they were gonna be doin' at a City Halls gig. Later Gerry and I got talkin' and played *In My Life* together in the dressing room and that was the beginning of what has been a long-standing friendship. I also had a few new songs from my stint in Denmark and they went on to my first album, for Decca. I had played on an album with BARBARA DICKSON and ARCHIE FISHER and they used three of my songs. Then I did my own album *(1970)*.

STEALERS WHEEL: Gerry brought Joe Egan along to some gig I was at in Glasgow *(1970/71)* and we were all singin' in the back of the van. When we said our goodbyes, Gerry mentioned putting a group together. He lived in Tonbridge Wells and in February 1971 I went to stay there. Then Joe and his wife came down and there was a Baby Grand piano in the room. We just sat and played music and I've never experienced anything like it. We would sing for hours and creativity was there. You walked in the room and felt like singin'!

But I was keen on performing and Gerry wasn't as keen. We did a few things . . . Roger Brown was involved . . . the LINDISFARNE connection provided interest from Tony Stratton Smith but that came to nothing . . . then RAY WILLIAMS and RICOCHET came into the picture. He had worked for DJM but the new operation didn't appear terribly competent and it got to the point that I didn't want to sign their management contract. And we were sitting around doing nothing for too long. I wanted to get out and play, although there were many times afterwards I looked back at the autumn of 1971 and wondered whether I denied myself access to something.

Gerry really wanted to write songs, make records and sculpt things. He's great at harmonies and technical things and he's also a good performer with a lot of presence, but it's no' really the place he wants to be. So I said I didn't want to sign a

JOE EGAN & GERRY RAFFERTY ROCK GARDEN

management contract and yet I allowed the same people to set up recording contracts for me.

Ricochet set up deals with A&M Records for both STEALERS WHEEL and myself. I was supposed to work with Lieber and Stoller as well. Unfortunately, the meeting was arranged with Mike Stoller and had it been with Jerry Lieber I might have got on all right. The first thing Stoller did was to play me one of their songs and then he said, "I think you could make a good job of this." *(Laughter)* I said, "I think I'll go back to my beer, thank you."

Bob Johnston (ex Bob Dylan producer) produced the A&M album I did, and it was all done quite live. He had come across to do two Charisma albums – by LINDISFARNE and BELL AND ARC – and he was happy to do something with me: Lindisfarne had done one of my songs on their first album and one on the second, and the Newcastle guys were really among the best people I had met as I toured. A&M then decided that I didn't have much American potential – the record was folky/country music – but when Larry Yaskiel moved to Warner Brothers, he took me with him.

Elliot Mazer was my next choice of producer, which was good the first time and bad the second. I had really liked the noise on *Harvest (by NEIL YOUNG)* and he had also done AREA CODE 615 and that clinched it because I wanted to go to Nashville and they agreed. *Red Pump Special* was the first album and I liked the way that turned out. I decided to work with him again and *Never Too Late* was the second.

Again I missed an opportunity at that time. I was in California on the Warners label in 1974 and two days into the second album with Elliot Mazer when he got a phone call from the CROSBY, STILLS, NASH AND YOUNG lot asking him to record a few shows on the road. So he put all his studio into his mobile unit and pissed off for four weeks, leaving me hanging about. What I should have done . . . I mean, I shouldn't have gone back to Mazer in the first place but, in the circumstances I now found myself, I should have gone to Mo Austin *(head of WB)* in LA. But I didn't know who I was meetin' when I was standing in that office and he introduced me to Lowell George and said, "Here's the guitar player from one of our bands, LITTLE FEAT." If I had known what was on tap at that time I could've probably made a record with COODER and the Little Feat people.

The whole thing became tense and difficult . . . I should've gone with a house producer, Russ Titelman or Lenny Waronker or someone, and allowed them to put something around me like the MARIA MULDAUR album. That was a missed opportunity. There were singles from *Red Pump Special* but I was in the US when they were coming out in the UK. Maybe the product wasn't there but at the same time, there were business strategies which were wrong.

Eventually I received an eloquent letter from Derek Taylor *(Warners, ex-Beatles PA)* dropping me from the label and thereafter I had to really work for a living. Unfortunately, I remained outspoken and was drinking too much although there were three more albums – *Restless (1977/78)* for Ringo's label which was done with Terry Melcher at Lennon's house, *Rab Noakes*, on MCA and *Under the Rain* which was done independently.

Now, all this time I had done a lot of radio work and enjoyed it as I had probably learned more from radio than any other source in my life. In 1985 I began doing programmes for Radio Scotland and, following a stint in Manchester, I have returned to Glasgow as Executive Producer, Entertainment.'

CHAPTER NINE

PETE AGNEW

'Could ye no' dae a gig in Downin' Street?'

NAZARETH were the first Dunfermline musicians to achieve national and international success and BARBARA DICKSON, ALAN DARBY, the SKIDS and BIG COUNTRY were soon to follow. Nazareth was financed in the international market initially by a Scottish bingo millionaire but completely justified his faith by scoring hits all over the world.

When I met Pete Agnew, late in 1990, Nazareth had just returned from a six-week tour of eastern Europe. This included ten nights at the Olympic Stadium in Moscow *(20,000 capacity, no support)*, 12 nights in Leningrad with a similar nightly capacity, five nights in Georgia and a trip to Lithuania where, apparently, the band is particularly popular and was greeted by a brass band on its arrival. Mr Gorbachev, who had been in Vilnius shortly before, did not receive as enthusiastic a welcome.

'I was born in 1946 and raised as a Catholic in Dunfermline. My great grandparents were Irish – there's a small Catholic population in the town – and St Margaret's School was for the entire area. All my Protestant pals were in classes o' 25. I was in a class o' 45!

There was always music at family get-togethers, some Irish music, and apparently my uncles played instruments, although I never saw them. My mother had been a dancer in the Opera House in Dunfermline, and where I learned harmonies was wi' her and my dad singin' things like *When It's Springtime In The Rockies*.

The first stuff I ever listened to was when we got a second-hand radiogram and some 78s which came with it. BING CROSBY was my dad's big favourite and I always enjoyed Bing and Gary Crosby. We were never a Sinatra family! Then I heard TENNESSEE ERNIE FORD doin' *My Hobby* and that was the closest to anythin' that half turned me on. There was a guitar in it for a start, and SLIM WHITMAN wi' *China Doll* and *Indian Love Call*. But it really arrived wi' PRESLEY. Ah wis nine or ten and that was when I wanted a guitar. Then I heard LITTLE RICHARD – an' he was just amazin'. And you didn't have to work that hard to get up to a standard where you could impress your friends at parties. Same as the punk thing.

The first guy I ever sat beside in a school was Dan McCafferty – Billy McCafferty as he was then – an' he gret aw day! Him an' I always liked the same music. After the skiffle thing I was in a group called the SPITFIRES wi' a Dettol can for a bass, playin' Buddy Holly an' we won the under 15s Fife skiffle competition at the Regal *(ABC)* in Kirkcaldy in 1956. I just sang at that time an' ignored what was happening behind me. Some of the other groups played chords but we won because we wore tartan shirts an' blue jeans! We should have been thrown oot! Anyway, later I used to run aboot wi' Dan – go up to his house and listen to Presley, but Dan wasn't actually in the first band which had a whole loada names. Manny *(Charlton)* at this time was in the MARK 5 then the RED HAWKS and the original Red Hawks were my idols . . . they used tae have the Red Hawks Twist Club at the Kinema *(Ballroom)*. It had nae bar and that's a pity for kids nowadays because aw the bands play in pubs. When I was 14 *(1960)* I started the SHADETTES *(which eventually evolved into NAZARETH)* and we played at the Valleyfield Institute and the Burntisland Palais. By 1960/63 we were the resident band and, before the BEATLES, we played the SHADOWS an' everybody. At the Ingle Neuk in Perth we played for five hours so everybody played different instruments tae gie the boy a break, an' a lot o' instrumentals tae save the voices. I was singer and rhythm guitarist, an' Dan was a mate o' the band, gettin' aw the women!

Around 1963, our drummer left and there was a wee guy I had seen playin' around Burntisland, who sometimes played wi' us on Saturday nights. This was Daryll *(Sweet)* and his singer, Des Haldane, also joined us for harmonies. Des played guitar, so I went on tae vocals. After about a year an' a half . . . I was workin' in an architect's office . . . he phoned me up just before we were due to play at the Place in Edinburgh to say he was leavin'. We struggled through the gig and, comin' back, somebody said, "What aboot Dan?" On the Saturday we were doin' Kirkcaldy YM which was a good gig, so we sat up all the Friday night goin' through half-a-dozen songs wi' Dan. He had the job if the yella suit fitted him! The first song was *Hi Heeled Sneakers* an' when the band came in, he just stood there! But he got on all right afterwards and later we moved on to soul music.

In 1966, we got a job in the Bellville in Dunfermline and started our own club, the Flamingo, where we did Stax with two vocals. At that time the PATHFINDERS and the BEATSTALKERS were big draws but the POETS were the greatest band – both the first group that played original material and the second that did covers.

Derek Nicol was originally from Rosyth and ran an agency oot o' his faither's plumber's shop. He got on well wi' everybody and would send us tae some quite tough places . . . Auchterarder, the Stardust in Rosyth . . . then he went to work for

*PETE AGNEW &
DAN McCAFFERTY
(1968)* PETE AGNEW

Andy Lothian in Dundee for a few years. By 1968 we had changed our name to Nazareth and were down to a four-piece. We sent Derek some tapes and he liked the songs. He also said he was moving to Music and Cabaret *(see RONNIE SIMPSON)* and this helped us get into their work. Derek was puntin' the stuff and around 1970 he was approached by this guy, Bill Fehilly, who ran a bingo company called Top Flight Leisure, from Perth. Bill had been a promoter previously and wanted to get back into the entertainment business. He had seen a ballad singer in Birmingham and wanted Andy Lothian to promote him with Bill's money. Andy by this time, though, had moved into insurance and put him in touch with Derek Nicol who looked at the guy and said, "Fair enough, but I think you should listen to Nazareth." He saw us at the Burns Howff and by the next week had decided to go with us. We weren't sure at first. We wanted to make a record but we had families and were in good jobs. I was an architect's technician, Dan was a mechanical engineer, Manny a radar technician and Daryll a chartered accountant.

But Derek wanted us to take the chance and we thought we would give it a year. We got a wage – £40 a week – and made the first album before we had a record deal. We recorded at Trident Studios where ELTON JOHN was recording, then signed with B&C which was an offshoot of Charisma. None of us had really made proper records before – hardly anyone from Scotland had been in a proper studio – and it took a fortnight. The trouble then was, they wanted every album to be made in a fortnight after that!

Fehilly always had pocketfuls of money and never put a limit on what he was prepared to spend on us, although we had the scuddiest flat I'd ever seen any band in. We went home as often as we could but we were on tour *all the time.* Playin' for three months in Britain, three months in Germany. The other two hard-workin' groups were RORY GALLAGHER and STATUS QUO. Wherever we were asked to play, if they had been before we were okay. In 1973 we did something like 280 dates and two albums. At that time, that was how you broke. It's no' so easy for bands now . . . SIMPLE MINDS is the only other Scottish one ah can think ae.

When we went out with DEEP PURPLE in the States . . . Fehilly had wanted us to play in America . . . we were in a hotel in Ayr one Friday night and Kansas City the next. We thought, this is no' bad, but if we'd known what Kansas was like, we'd have gone back to Ayr! We were third on the bill . . . DEEP PURPLE, BUDDY MILES an' us, and we'd had to pay money to share in the PA. Bill saw our real big hit goin' into the charts *(Love Hurts, number seven US, 1976)* but by the time we were headlining he was dead in a plane crash.'

On the point of Fehilly's money making the hits . . .

'Usually it's the record companies that bankroll the groups but record companies didnae really want tae know aboot Scottish groups. And we had tae get a hit . . . I mean, ZEPPELIN'S money was behind STONE THE CROWS, but they couldna' do anythin'. After the second album, we were told that this was the last year of bein' full-time. Luckily, we *knew* we had a hit album next time around. We had been writin' an' doin' the tracks from *Razamanaz* live, rhythm and blues, and we knew we had the ingredients.

Funnily enough, Bill didn't want to know. He said, "You can record one track and we'll see." We did *Broken Down Angel* because we thought it was the "pop" one. But we had others and we talked him into an album. We got a mobile studio, took it to a warehouse in Inverkeithing and did it in ten days! It was a monster and cost 30 bob! *(1973).*

Then they began to look at other bands and Bill's death left us in a hole because we still owed money to his estate. So they sold the Mountain label to us with Derek at the helm and we ran it from 1976 until 1980, when it collapsed. It was

bad management because we were doing 20,000 seaters in the States, but expenses *NAZARETH with* had got out of hand. We came back from one tour which had grossed £1½ million *ZAL CLEMINSON* and were told it was successful because we had only lost 80 grand! We got cars and PETE AGNEW houses but never cash in hand . . . and there were a lot of daft projects, bands that had no chance. Havin' said that, I loved the ALEX HARVEY BAND and the SLEAZ BAND. Fehilly hated them *(Sleaz Band)* because they never took him seriously, and they never got a chance to record. I still see Jim Brodie *(singer)*. He's a union leader in Toronto.

The company never went second class. They ended up in Mayfair when a telephone would have looked after Nazareth . . . £36,000 a year for an office to rent! By the time we wised-up it was too late and we've had to work off a million pounds. But now we have so many albums . . . 20 or so . . . and we're well-known all over the world . . .

NAZARETH
PETE AGNEW
We were in the Philippines just before Marcos was overthrown . . . we were in India just before Mrs Gandhi was killed . . . aboot the time o' the miners' strike some o' ma minin' pals were sayin' . . . "Could ye no' dae a gig in Downin' Street?!" Also I reckon that I've spent somethin' like eight or nine years o' ma life on tour in America.'

ALAN DARBY

'Improvising . . . but keeping it together'

ALAN DARBY is one of those musicians who appeared to enter the profession 'fully formed'. Even in his earliest days with the group CADO BELLE, he was a technician par excellence and with a feel which would make the very best blues-based players look to their laurels. He remains one of the great 'undiscovered' players in rock music, although recent touring and recording work with ROBERT PALMER and PAUL YOUNG may have begun to alter that. He was born in Dunfermline in 1952, the son of a civil servant, and attended Dunfermline High and Edinburgh University, where he took a degree in Civil Engineering.

'I used to play acoustic stuff with friends, then at 14 I heard the JOHN MAYALL/ERIC CLAPTON album, *Bluesbreakers*. We started a band called the NEW BROOM BLUES BAND and played at school dances doing all the tracks from the *Bluesbreakers* album and *A Hard Road*. CLAPTON, PETER GREEN and MICK TAYLOR – they were the guys who were doin' it and, it's funny, I've come back to this recently.

At school I wasn't really that good at anything, I just worked hard. I failed my 11-plus and went to this junior high school where they did things like cobbling and gardening *(joke)*. The best that it could lead to was an apprenticeship at Rosyth dockyard. I saw what my older sister was doing and thought, "I don't like this." So I went to night school and got some 'O' grades. At university – I only really went because my friends went – it was one of those things where you think you've got to cover yourself. Anyway, I met Alastair Robertson, he had a Wurlitzer piano and we had a jam in the halls of residence. Then he said he knew these people in Glasgow – the idea was to bring STUART MacKILLOP and MAGGIE REILLY who were in one band, together with COLIN TULLY, GAVIN HODGSON and DAVY ROY, who were in another. We got together for a jam in Colin's flat in Gibson Street, and I thought they were all good players . . . it obviously had some potential. The group became CADO BELLE and we played around Scotland at first . . . full-time, but signing-on as well.

By 1976 there was growing national interest in the group and we were signed to Anchor Records. We did an album with a guy called Keith Olsen producing – he had recently come from working with FLEETWOOD MAC – but then the punk thing happened, the record company went broke, and we had internal problems. Perhaps if we had gone to America, it might have lasted longer. I was listening to people like LARRY CARLTON and the CRUSADERS.

95

KIM BEACON

I remember latterly it was very hard work . . . for gigs like the Music Machine in Camden Town I used to have to pick up a hired car at seven in the morning, drive to London, unload the gear, do the gig, put it back in the truck, then drive back to Glasgow because we didn't have money for hotels or extra car-hire. I remember going up the motorway with Gavin sitting beside me saying, "Are you sleeping, Alan?" I still sometimes play with Gavin.

After that, I went to Berkeley Jazz school in Boston for three or four months. Andy Park at Radio Clyde had a number of scholarships and it was a great experience although musically a bit boring – too academic. I prefer things that have got "feel" – it goes back to the blues thing. I decided I didn't want to be a jazz player, but when I came home I did a concert with some of the guys – some original stuff plus a Celtic thing with the WHISTLEBINKIES and EDDIE McGUIRE.

By then I had virtually done everything I could in Scotland. I did a thing with a singer, KIM BEACON, who I thought was brilliant, but it was short-lived – more one-off trips to London etc. By then Maggie Reilly and Colin Tully were both doing well – Maggie worked with MIKE OLDFIELD – and Stuart was getting involved in tour management.

I just went with the flow . . . I did an album with LES McKEOWN, and a tour of Japan, then *Tommy* in the West End. After that I did nothing for two or three years – I worked in a cocktail bar in Covent Garden. I briefly joined up with BOBBY TENCH *(from JEFF BECK GROUP)*, JERRY SHIRLEY *(HUMBLE PIE)*, CHARLIE WHITNEY *(FAMILY)* and CHARLIE McCRACKEN *(TASTE)*, and we did some recordings, but tended to get plastered all the time.

I got a flat with Frances *(long-time girlfriend)* in Shepherds Bush, worked with STEVE HARLEY for a couple of years, then I joined FASHION. TROY TATE was the singer but he left, and Muff Winwood who had heard some of my demos more or less thrust me into the position of singing. I can sing a bit now, but then . . . it was fun. Rock'n'roll, drugs and crazy women . . . It was a trendy band, with a strong image and cult following, and I was listening to ADRIAN BELEW. We toured the UK and Germany and made one album, *Twilight of Idols*, for CBS.

Then I got a solo deal with Siren, which was part of Virgin, and did an album in America, which wasn't released. Cost 190 grand or something. They saw me as a cross between ERIC CLAPTON and BILLY IDOL/ . . . Eric Idle? *(laughs)* whom I know! I recorded in LA and lived there for four months, which was interesting but lonely as I was on my own and the producer was married. They released a single which never made the Radio One playlist and that was the end of that. At least I saw some money, and I bought another flat in Shepherds Bush.

I joined BONNIE TYLER after that; we did a tour and went to Russia for six weeks. Interesting. I heard some folk stuff which was amazing. Then through Frances I got a call from ROBERT PALMER and I met him when he was doing a video for *Simply Irresistible* with the photographer, Terence Donovan. It was into the limo and down to the St James' Club, where we got blind drunk. He asked me to do a tour – the Far East, Australia and Japan – so I went to Australia to rehearse, then toured Hawaii, Singapore, Guam . . . It was amazing and musically just great, although the band contained some extreme personalities – like FRANK BLAIR. He used to get arrested and stuff but was the most amazing bass player I've ever heard. He used to play with MARVIN GAYE, and I just listened to him most nights . . . improvising, but keeping it together.

The problem was, I had a relationship with a girl who was also in the band and that carried on until I started working with PAUL YOUNG – when everything began to fall apart – again! Anyway, I usually look at three things – the music, the money and the personalities involved – although sometimes you don't know what you're doing. I mean, at one point I was thinking about giving it up altogether, and I ran into MICHAEL MacDONALD who was over here. He told me he'd been through something similar, and was thinking of giving up singing!'

Far Left: CADO BELLE

Left: ALAN DARBY
ALAN DARBY

97

THE SKIDS Richard *Jobson, 1st left* ROCK GARDEN

RICHARD JOBSON BBC SCOTLAND

RICHARD JOBSON
'. . . a particularly despairing future'

RICHARD JOBSON has graduated from a punk rock partnership with STUART ADAMSON in the SKIDS, to art rock with the ARMOURY SHOW, and more recently, fashion modelling and TV presentation.

'In the Seventies I became interested in the glitzy glam music of DAVID BOWIE, T REX and MOTT THE HOOPLE. Then Punk happened and I found myself quite attracted to the more social aspects – how they dressed and carried on. I had only read about it in newspapers, but I was the only one in Dunfermline. STUART ADAMSON had a kind of R&B band and they were looking for someone who looked right to be the singer. It was nothing to do with musical talent.

I come from an Irish Catholic background, so there were always those sentimental ballads in the family which I suppose I attached myself to. The family moved around Fife – my father was a coalminer – so we were very working class. Five boys in a two-roomed tenement, so there wasn't a lot of money around. My oldest brother was interested in music – wild stuff like FRANK ZAPPA, CAPTAIN BEEFHEART and a bit of jazz – and that was my introduction to music, but the SKIDS was just great energy. There were no socio-political ideas, just a tremendous enthusiasm to do with havin' a great time with a bunch of people I liked. Stuart used to write everything . . . then I started writing lyrics . . . although they were a bit abstract and didn't make much sense.

We started an independent record company called No' Bad Records and No' Bad One was called *Charles* which Stuart wrote *(1978)* and I still think it's a good song now. By that time we had started to get a bit of attention from John Peel on Radio 1, which led to some record company interest. Then we started to play in Edinburgh a bit more when some of the English bands were comin' up and playin' here. We were quite aggressive kids, and we would wait until the main act arrived and say, "Can we be third on the bill?" We had nothing to lose, and our management consisted of a local biker looking after us – a Hell's Angel.

Quite soon after that, Virgin Records picked us up for not very much money. It was a scandalous deal, really, and I still suffer from it. They cross-collateralised between the record deal and the publishing – so either way they got their money, and we didn't make any money. And we sold a phenomenal amount of records. But

99

we were never managed properly, and when we did get management, we were beyond manipulation. Around the end of 1980, we just drifted off and did our own things.

It could have gone on and been tremendous, because the combination of Stuart and me was terrific. Musically, he had stumbled on a sound and it worked with my voice. We also always liked the traditional thing. I was more of an Irishman, Stuart was very Scottish . . . very patriotic, nationalistic. We connected on the sentimentality.

I left school at 16, but I was always interested in reading and writing, and I began to develop that during the SKIDS period because I had more and more time on my own. I wouldn't go back to music now, because first of all I wasn't a musician and so I found it very frustrating trying to make ideas concrete. I didn't have the musical means and whereas I had a relationship with Stuart, it was difficult to explain things to others. Stuart and I combined well because he understood what I was trying to say. Everyone else I tried to combine with since then has been a disaster, but I think there's a fear of going back to what I came from, so I've just found myself working all the time.

What's going on in broadcasting right now is quite exciting. I don't think you have to come from an academic background, and the idea of having to have a posh English accent to work in the BBC has gone now . . . although still not in the Arts, sadly. It's still manipulated by those kind of people, but I think their days are numbered. There's a whole new generation of aggressive, still angry people . . . I still retain that anger. For me, *(punk)* meant a chance to escape from a particularly despairing future, and find other interests. I've never been a particularly flamboyant person because I'm so aware of social injustice. I come from that situation and I go back to it constantly, to see my family. I try to maintain some kind of dignity.

In certain areas, the doors are still closed, but I have a good job in London *(Thames TV presenter)* . . . I get the opportunity to talk about painting, theatre. It gives your normal punter – which I am – a chance to voice an opinion. In music, for example, I'm interested in why people continue to do it. It fascinates me, and there's always an energy when it's honest. Although, both in Glasgow and London, I find a lot of people who are only doing it to add to their bank balance, which I find really depressing. That's what happened towards the end of the Skids. We were writing for our bank accounts rather than our hearts.'

CHAPTER TEN

MAE MCKENNA

'Sing soft . . . but loud'

MAE McKENNA was born in Coatbridge in 1955, into a family of great musical talent. Her father played accordion in a band with his brothers which toured Scotland and Ireland, before moving into variety theatres; her mother sang professionally and later studied at the Scottish Royal Academy; her father's sisters had a singing act; her maternal grandmother was the music-hall singer, May Melby; her brother Hugh and cousin Ted played with the SENSATIONAL ALEX HARVEY BAND among others; another brother and another cousin both have musical careers; and a cousin, Jeannie Lamb, was the original CLYDE VALLEY STOMPERS' vocalist. The list goes on.

'We were speaking about home quite recently and PAT DOYLE remarked about the fact that such an incredible amount of talent had come out of that little patch of Lanarkshire, between Uddingston, Coatbridge and Airdrie.

Both sets of grandparents came from Ireland, my father's people from Monaghan and my mother's from Armagh, and I have a picture of my grandmother on sheet music. When my father was in the house, he played the piano all the time . . . on a Sunday for six hours, so music never disturbs me, if neighbours are playing it, or whatever. It was always in the background and I just shut it out. People can be playing drums . . . I filter it out.

My mother trained as a singer and always maintains that a voice should never be trained until the age of 17. Apparently, I could sing in tune at the age of two, and when I started to tinkle about on the piano *(four)*, my father taught me to read. But I always liked to do things myself. I took up violin when I was seven or eight then went on to viola, and soon after, when I joined the Lanarkshire Youth Orchestra *(14)*, I met the first band. It was called DAY and included the aforementioned Patrick Doyle *(composer of music for Kenneth Branagh's* Henry V*)* and a guy called Paul McGuire, who was a bit older than us and whose music it was we played. Sort of INCREDIBLE STRING BAND *(1968/69)*. I was also hearing things that Hugh liked at this time, MOTOWN and CREAM.

At a festival in Uddingston, I was seen by George and Billy Jackson who had a FAIRPORT-style folk group called CONTRABAND. However, I was wearing a peculiar green velvet cloak with a hood and they were apparently put off by this . . . but I met them later in Glasgow when I was more "normally" dressed, and they asked me to join the band. This would be around 1970 and I was still at school, listening to JONI MITCHELL and SANDY DENNY. We worked for a promoter called Andy Daisley and we did a tour with BILLY CONNOLLY at one stage.

In 1973, we won a *Melody Maker* competition and were offered a deal with Transatlantic in London. They found us a flat in Hendon and we moved around the turn of the year *(1973/74)*. I had gone straight from school, but my parents had no objections. We lasted for about another year as CONTRABAND *(George, Billy, John Martin and Peter Cairney)* but then musical differences began to develop, and I went on to a solo deal. I made three albums over the next couple of years and one – *Everything That Touches Me* – cleared my debt with the company. At one point I wanted to leave Transatlantic, but they insisted I fulfil my contract and I kind of drifted away from that type of career.

In 1978, I got a job in the chorus of *Jesus Christ Superstar*. I was part of a gospel trio and we were seen by a number of producers, one of whom, Adam Kidron, asked us to do the first SCRITTI POLITTI album. Sessions then began to come out of that and I started to do vocal arrangements which producers also noticed. I did some gospel choir arrangement for Adam as well, and I could always sing harmony. From a very early age. I could hear the chords whether or not they were there so, once I'd heard the tune, the harmonies would be there in my head. People would start asking for the "Scritti Girls" and I just drifted into it the way I've done with everything else in my life. I didn't think I wanted to be in another band because, although in CONTRABAND we got on very well personally, and still do, musical differences crop up and I didn't want to be in a situation where you were arguing over musical direction again.

I was married in 1977. Kim is Malaysian and I met him at a karate class! We have a little boy, Jamie, and he had a musical ear at a very early age.'

SESSIONS:

'It's funny, some of the sessions I thought were great, the records didn't even come out. We did one for STING once, for a film – *I Need Your Love So Bad* – I really liked that but it didn't appear. And there was a guitarist who later worked with DAVID BOWIE – KEVIN ARMSTRONG – we did some of his solo tracks about eight years ago and I can still remember one tune, even although I never heard it again. Beyond that there was IAN DURY, WET WET WET, ABC and, for the last seven years or so, all the STOCK AITKEN AND WATERMAN stuff. In fact, there's hardly been a day in that time that I haven't been in a studio.

The three girls had done work with a German producer called Zeus B. Held, and he did DEAD OR ALIVE's first album, which we sang on. They then moved to STOCK AITKEN AND WATERMAN and asked for us. I was pregnant with Jamie *(1982/ 83)*, and I've been with them ever since . . . KYLIE MINOGUE – it's teenage music, not what I'd buy, but she has talent. She has a good ear and sings harmonies with us sometimes. Plus JASON DONOVAN, DONNA SUMMER, RICK ASTLEY etc. I also do a lot of work for jingle companies. There are maybe eight female singers and the same number of guys who do the majority of session work in London and one guy –

LANCE ELLINGTON – has a solo career like myself, as well.

It's quite a disciplined thing. You have to get there on time, be very quick, and you've got to listen to some bizarre instructions from advertising people like, "Sing soft . . . but loud". You have to take all this in patiently and then make them believe that that's what you're doing. The key, therefore, is picking up things quickly, coming out with ideas quickly and being versatile. I mean, some of the jingles I do don't involve pure singing at all – they're very raunchy. I can do a sort of BONNIE TYLER voice, which surprises people who think they know my voice! I did all the Tennents commercials, for example, with FRANKIE MILLER.

I listen to a broad range of music and I picked up on my own career again when a friend was moving house and he was looking for somewhere to store his 8-track studio. I started writing again and recording it and I thought, "Gosh, I really miss this!" It was quite folk-influenced stuff and when the guy came back – it was Julian Marshall of Marshall Hain – he said, "Why don't you do something with this?" So my manager, Keith Harris, took the tape to Virgin and they signed it. Now Virgin in Japan are going to do another one. I did a little tour with STEVE HACKETT – I thought I was going to be sick, going on stage again – but it went well and I enjoyed it. Musically, it's just an extension of the folk music I was doing 12 years ago, but incorporating all the other influences, and record company interest was really instant as soon as I went in that direction. Of course, I've also had to get into computer technology, but I combine this with acoustic instruments.

Right now, I like WENDY AND LISA, who worked with PRINCE – very interesting – MARIAH CAREY and SINEAD O'CONNOR. In the folk area I love DAVY SPILLANE – I think the Irish have taken things a stage farther than the Scots. They appear to be given more encouragement by their government and so forth. Although, potentially, there are plenty of people in Scotland who could do even better than that. But, of course, they don't have access to the studios in Scotland.'

CHAPTER ELEVEN

TAM WHITE

'. . . they put their equipment on a barra' and walked to London'

TAM WHITE'S *career has been a Scottish blues variation. After local success he went to London in the early Sixties. On his return he was subjected to the horrors of cabaret and* NEW FACES *although this gave him a minor hit record in the Seventies. In the Eighties he returned to his jazz/blues roots and this has led to appearances at Ronnie Scott's Club, more recording and some interesting television work* (Tutti Frutti, Wreck on the Highway).

'I was born in 1942 and brought up right in the centre of Edinburgh, in the Grassmarket. The city was a series of different communities in these days and the Grassmarket was the hub. All the carriers and horses coming from the station with goods to be distributed made it an exciting place to live in.

My mother came from the mining village of Gilmerton near Edinburgh and my father from the city itself. He was driver with the cleansing department all his life and I've got one sister who was also involved in music. It came really from my mother's side, although my father liked music and we had a piano.

My mother's grandfather had been a bandleader with nine sons, all of whom played. My sister and I were sent for piano lessons but to walk through the streets with a music book under your arm was considered sissy, so being working class had its drawbacks as far as music was concerned. I stuck it for three years and could play by ear but couldn't read sheet music. My sister was the opposite: she passed the exams.

Then I started off in the folk thing. My mother's mother used to sing at OAP dos and it was all Scottish songs which she would write down in a jotter. So I was brought up on the Scottish songs like *Westering Home* and *Bonnie Mary of Argyll* and I ended up going to Sandy Bell's pub in Edinburgh with a skiffle group. We were one of the first groups to play there and I had become a BUDDY HOLLY fan so it was a strange mixture we played: rock'n'roll and Scottish material like *The Road To Dundee* and *Scots Wha Hae.'*

Folk purists may now turn in their graves. Sandy Bell's pub enjoys celebrity as one of the cradles of the Fifties Scottish folk music revival.

'Two of the boys stayed above the pub. One played guitar and the other a sort of snare and cymbal. I sang and the fourth guy came from Marchmont. He was "lead guitarist" since he knew aboot four chords! I still see a couple of them around Edinburgh.

At secondary school . . . I was at Darroch in Gilmore Place . . . they had light opera and I got involved in that: *The Student Prince* and *The Beggars' Opera*. I was offered an audition with the Edinburgh Opera Company but turned it down and I was never interested in the academic thing . . .

But I did become interested in the blues. When I was 16 I started going to this seedy drinking club, the Berkeley in Lothian Road, and US servicemen from the Kirknewton base used to drink there. I got chattin' to a couple of black guys and they gave me records by MUDDY WATERS and JIMMY WITHERSPOON. I particularly liked Witherspoon because he wasn't strictly 12-bar. It was a wee bit classier and jazzier. So I got involved in that but it was difficult in the late Fifties to find a band that was interested in that kind of music. Most bands played pop or covers of country singers like JIM REEVES, PAT BOONE or PRESLEY. I was never that keen on Presley.

Then, I think I saw ALEX HARVEY in the dance hall down in Leith. I forget the name of it but the band impressed me and I got to know the guys later, in London. And, of course, I was a fan of RAY CHARLES and he started doing country music, so I did too. Why not, if you like it?

Eventually, I got a job with a guy from Heriot's school called Bill Mulholland. He had a band called the DEAN HAMILTON COMBO and the drummer, TOTO *(McNaughton)* got me the gig. I had tried to start a BUDDY HOLLY thing with him before.

The band had a good set-up. They played church halls, Scout and BB dances – all non-profit making places – but there were no clubs then *(1958/59)* so I worked with them for a year and a half. Then a late night coffee bar opened in Fishmarket Close, off the High Street, called the Gamp Club.

It was Brian Waldman who ran it and he later became my manager before going to London and, eventually, starting the Middle Earth club which became a famous psychedelic venue. He was a Londoner himself and a few years older than me and, actually, I used to cause a bit of trouble in his place . . . just boisterousness through drink . . . so he ended up givin' me a gig there and this led to the BOSTON DEXTERS.

He dreamed up the idea. It came from the Damon Runyon books and Brian

BOSTON DEXTERS
M. MacNAUGHTON

saw it as a band that was also a gang. Toto was a very funny guy . . . and we dressed up as gangsters. It was in the early Sixties and created good press. The music was RAY CHARLES, MOSE ALLISON, BOBBY BLAND and Glasgow's BLUES COUNCIL was in a similar mould. We did a residency with them, every Sunday for a year at the Place in Victoria Street, which was also Waldman's club.

There were a lot of bands in Edinburgh by then . . . the ABSTRACTS, the NIGHTSHIFT, SHANE AND THE SABRES, the DOMINOES . . . and the MARK FIVE who made a bit of a stir by walking to London to get on *Ready Steady Go (TV rock show)*. Scottish bands couldn't get on the programme so they put their equipment on a barra' and walked to London! They made an appearance . . . they were marched on and marched off without playin'! But they did get some kind of deal, with Bunny Lewis.

The DEXTERS were full-time. I did an apprenticeship first. I'm a stonemason to trade and I did it until I was 21. Then I was full-time in music for 16 years. I still enjoy the masonry, though, and in an ideal world if I was makin' enough money from music, I would keep a wee shed at the bottom of the garden for stone work. It's a craft, really.

The BOSTON DEXTERS went south in 1964. We were offered a deal with Joe Meek but Waldie didn't fancy that and took us to Columbia instead. It was a bad mistake because the song that Meek had earmarked for us was *Please Stay*. Anyway, we lost that and made a couple of terrible records with Columbia. Bill Martin was involved and it was the old story. Everyone wanted us to sound like the BEATLES and, at that age, we were dependin' on the advice of others. The A-sides were pop things and the B-sides, songs like *I Believe To My Soul*. Two entirely different things.

Waldman had another club in London – the Putney Pontiac – and we played support for all the bands . . . MANFRED MANN, LONG JOHN BALDRY. ALEX HARVEY'S band would do that gig and we lived in a flat above the place, so there would be a big shindig afterwards.

During the psychedelic time I got into some folk-rock things . . . TIM HARDIN and LEONARD COHEN . . . just guitar and voice and, when I came back to Edinburgh, I played around the Old Town pubs. I had had other deals in London . . . with Decca/ Deram and again with Joe Meek but the records were naff. I was also in Jersey for a wee while but, basically, I had lost my way. Decca wanted me to be TOM JONES, with Deram I did a CAROLE KING song, *Old Sweet Roll* . . . so I came home, began doing working men's clubs and . . . things got worse.

I was on the *Tommy Makem Show* at STV and they offered me a series so it was . . . hair cut off, dickie bow tie . . . and I did 21 shows in the early Seventies. Of course, it was down to me. No one twisted my arm and I always thought if I could get a foothold with one thing, I could then change to something else. But you can never do that. You're up there selling something you don't believe in and it shows. However, I had a minor hit record.

In clubland, I ended up with an MC job at the Bird's Cage in Edinburgh and DAVE PRINGLE, who was the keyboard player, moved as MD to *New Faces* and offered me a spot. I did it, was signed by Mickie Most and released *What In The World's Come Over You,* a Jack Scott song that became a Top 40 hit. I think Mickie Most was a bit off the boil by then, though.

Anyway, I was then offered a job in CCS by John Cameron who wanted me to replace ALEXIS KORNER, but the management company didn't want me to do it and I thought everything was all over.

I went back to the trade *(late Seventies)* and it was very difficult having done television shows and everything but it was a good thing for me and kind of levelled me out.

When I began missing playing, I started doing the guitar and voice thing again

and next I was offered an album by Colin Chisholm and Brian Spence of BILBO BAGGINS. This took me to the States for six weeks and, although people weren't too keen on the material, they liked the voice and I came back rejuvenated.

I was offered a job in Norway *(1980)* but, unfortunately, although I had been sober for a year, as soon as I left the house I got pissed and blew the gig. I ended up in jail in Norway, skint, and the only thing I had was the phone number of Bill Mulholland *(formerly of the DEAN HAMILTON COMBO)* who had settled over there. So he took me in for a few days and he still played guitar, so he wanted to do a couple of gigs in a reputable place in Oslo . . . the Hothouse.

The material we knew was blues . . . and it was the best two nights I'd had in 20 years! I thought, "That's it, man, I've been wasting my time." I realised that I was involved in music because I loved doin' it, and we blew the place apart. I said to

109

the club owner, "What time do we start playin'?" and he said, "Whenever you feel like it."

So I decided to do that back home. I worked with the guitarist JIM CONDIE and it built up into a band which we called the DEXTERS. People of my age came and so did their kids. And I have catholic musical tastes so we played a pretty varied programme. I've been doin' folk festivals this year with FRASER SPIERS *(harmonica)*.

But the next thing was *Tutti Frutti (BBC TV)*. I had been workin' for BBC Radio and I bumped into Andy Park who was producin' the John Byrne series. He liked what we were doin' and I ended up doin' the singin' voice of Big Jazza *(Robbie Coltrane)*. By that stage, though, I was ready to leave the band to do more of my own material. I felt I should have something to say for myself after everything I'd been through. Actually, it was one of my own songs that won the *New Faces* thing but I wasn't properly into writin' then.

Then there was a band comin' up here that featured BOZ BURRELL *(ex-BAD COMPANY)* and someone had suggested to him that we get together. I sang a couple of numbers and we got on well. I was just back from the States again – curiously, I had written a song when I was in Tennessee that the BBC later got a Nashville singer to do in *Wreck On The Highway* – and I was looking for something, so we started the BIG BAND. And again, funnily enough, the guitarist was IAN BAIRNSON *(PILOT)* who I had previously done Palais-type gigs with at Tiffany's in Edinburgh.

Now we've done Ronnie Scott's and recorded an album there, and the band's comin' up for an Edinburgh Festival gig at the Queen's Hall. It's a band for the Nineties and I don't want to do gigs that are not worthy of the musicians. In a way, it's become an obsession again.'

CHAPTER TWELVE

ALAN LONGMUIR

'Just greedy men . . .'

For all that they were a major commercial phenomenon, one of the biggest in pop music during the mid-Seventies, there is always a great temptation for people to 'rubbish' the BAY CITY ROLLERS. As purveyors of the ultimate youth image of the period, they achieved great success on both sides of the Atlantic, but emerged as victims of another image: puppet musicians, directed by a small-town Svengali to do whatever was necessary to get to the top, only to see the financial rewards cruelly commandeered by those more adept at playing the music business game.

'Just greedy men,' says ALAN LONGMUIR, succinctly describing the executives who control the recording and music publishing industries via accountants and lawyers. 'One accountant in particular, when £800 should have been an appropriate fee for an audit, took £8,000. That was the way it went.'
However one would wish to describe Alan Longmuir, now 41 years old and with a recently failed marriage and hotel business behind him, greed is not a concept with which he would have been familiar, growing up in Caledonian Road at Haymarket, in Edinburgh. He and his brother Derek, who were to form the backbone of the group, came from what was essentially a Highland family – from Easter Ross and Inverness – which had moved to Edinburgh during his grandparents' time and built up strong associations with the railways. Both sides of the family were musical and the boys and their two sisters grew up in a lively atmosphere of parties where uncles and their father played Scottish traditional music on the accordion.

'We went to Dalry Primary School and Tynecastle Senior Secondary. I didnae like school but I got my Edinburgh Schools Certificate and went to work as a clerk wi' the Co-op. I hated it and wanted to be an electrician, but there were no jobs. Somebody suggested plumbing, so I started an apprenticeship and attended night-school and day release at Napier College.'

At about this time Derek Longmuir also undertook an apprenticeship – as a joiner – but music had begun to play a more important role in their lives and with Alan developing an interest in playing the piano and accordion, his younger brother had taken up drums at the Boys' Brigade.

'My cousins used to go to the Scotia Picture House in Dalry Road. We went to see

Jailhouse Rock and they were dancin' in the aisles. I couldna' believe it! I wis aboot ten an' we started swingin' on the wardrobe door, practising jiving. I wanted to buy a guitar and the one I had my eye on cost £30, quite a lot of money. My father offered to stand guarantor if I kept on my milk round and papers. I paid ten bob a week an' played it upside doon *(left-handed)*.

Scott Murray was a guy whose family had a tool shop in Haymarket. He showed me the rudiments and when we were still at school we formed a band – the SAXONS – wi' my cousin Neil Porteous and Dave *(the Rave)* Pettigrew. We went to the Cairn Church in Gorgie Road where a guy from Boroughmuir School played. One time he was going to a wedding and we stood in with Nobby Clark, who was at school wi' Derek, singing. We played BEATLES songs and early TAMLA MOTOWN, and developed a little following *(1964/65)*.

After a while, Neil left and Greig Ellison came in. For a time we had two Vox organ players – Dave Pettigrew and Keith Norman – and two singers – Nobby and Mike Ellison, Greig's brother. Like the WALKER BROTHERS. We played the Cairn Church, Romano Bridge Hotel, and the Gonk Club at Tollcross. Derek was the quiet type and looked after the money, all of which went back into the band.'

> This, then, was the fairly traditional route for working-class boys. Most families would have had connections with churches, and the church hall circuit was important for the younger groups. Whereas the more academically inclined boys could only devote, say, a Sunday and a couple of evenings to rehearsal, the lad who had an apprenticeship or a job could throw himself wholeheartedly into rehearsal, every night if necessary. And since he also earned a small wage, he could afford to re-invest his group earnings. The SAXONS did just this and, trimmed down to a five-piece with one keyboard player (Norman) and one singer (Clark), they set about looking for better gigs and a manager.

'The Top Storey was a club at the top of Leith Walk where the St James Centre is today. It was run by the Craig brothers and Greig and myself went there, while Derek and Nobby tried somewhere else. Standing at the door was Tam Paton. I knew who he was but was scared to talk to him. He said, "Come and speak to me in the car."'

> Paton was the son of a potato merchant in Prestonpans. He was an accomplished pianist and accordionist who led the TOM PATON SHOWBAND and another top Edinburgh group, the CRUSADERS. On one occasion they supported the BEATLES and Paton approached Brian Epstein for his professional opinion as

112

to what was 'wrong' with the Edinburgh group. 'Image,' said the guru.

'Tam had discotheques and ran a wee club in Prestonpans. He also promoted gigs and had good contacts. Everybody knew him. There was a big thing for American names like MITCH RYDER and the DETROIT WHEELS. I thought "Rollers" had something going, so we stuck a pin in a map and, second time around it came out, Bay City, Michigan. Years later we got the keys to that city.

Paton agreed to come and audition the BAY CITY ROLLERS in the front room of the house in Caledonian Road, where we still rehearsed. He never turned up, however, so I phoned him. Eventually he came wi' Davie Paton – a great wee guy who was in a group called the BEACHCOMBERS – and their manager, Kenny MacLean. We were probably crap, but Paton saw five young laddies, keen as mustard, and decided to take us on. "They'll do f— all," said MacLean, later.'

Paton's idea, which owed much to Epstein's philosophy was, in Longmuir's words, to make the group 'untouchable'. They should not drink or associate with girlfriends. They should foster a clean image by working for charity. On stage, they should improve their presentation and, with the active support of his mother and father, he worked tirelessly (and honestly, in Longmuir's

113

opinion) for what he now saw as his special project. By the late Sixties the band had a sizeable following, although as an attraction as well as a musical group; they knew they still had a long way to go.

'The top groups were the Glasgow groups, the PATHFINDERS and the *(new)* POETS and we thought we'd never be as big as them. We did have a following, though. We played Rosewell Miners' Institute in Lasswade with ROBERT PLANT and his BAND OF JOY. He said, "How did you get a following like that?" Local guys, I suppose. Later on, we were there wi' the BEE GEES, and local promoters were beginning to bid against each other to get us. One New Year, we got £300.' *(At this time – 1968 – a chart group coming to Scotland would earn less than £200. CREAM were asking £300 for a university tour.)*

'We were pals wi' a lot o' the groups – LINNIE PATERSON and the JURY – but sometimes we got aggravation. Once we dressed up for a Charity Walk wi' Jimmy Savile, and when we got back to the Metropole Café in Torphichen Street where the groups went, some were sayin' – "Look at these arseholes!" Paton pulled out a wad of notes an' says, "No' bad for dressin' up as arseholes!"'

> At this time there was still no business arrangement or company to look after the band's interests. DEREK LONGMUIR still kept the money and the accounts. Things, however, were beginning to gear up. GREIG ELLISON was replaced by DAVIE PATON and KEITH NORMAN by BILLY LYALL. Both replacements would later form the chart-topping PILOT group.

'We played what the punters wanted. Harmony stuff, like CROSBY, STILLS AND NASH. We would play the Beach Ballroom in Aberdeen and there would be a bus fae Edinburgh – organised by the lassies themselves. Each member had his own following, and when we went on stage we wore suits and bow ties.

One night, we were playin' the Caves Club in Edinburgh. A guy called Tony Calder, who had been involved with Andrew Loog Oldham, was in Glasgow and couldn't get a plane back to London. Ronnie Simpson, the Glasgow agent, brought him over and, at one point, he was knocked doon the stair by screamin' lassies. He wanted to sign us, and offered an advance of £5,000 *(1970)*. At the same time, Dick Leahy, a genuine guy who has WHAM'S publishing, ran Bell Records and we signed with them. The £5,000 that Calder had promised us, though, was actually coming from Bell Records and, although we had a hit with *Keep On Dancin' (produced by Jonathan King),* we never saw a penny. Once the band was moving, we re-

negotiated the contract with Calder, and £100 got us off the hook.

    We did a few more songs, but they did nothing apart from one called *Mañana* which won a Luxembourg Grand Prix – we had no money, and SLADE bought us a drink, I remember – and we were going to be dropped by Bell. Then we came across Bill Martin and Phil Coulter, and they had the song *Remember*. Nobby sang on it originally but he was wanting to do his own songs, maybe as B-sides, and Martin and Coulter couldn't have this. It was all money. Nobby was writing good songs and fell out wi' Tam who was trying to keep the business momentum going. Both were right in their own way, and Nobby left which meant that we had to re-do the voice.

    LES McKEOWN was a bummer who was playin' in a wee band. He had been on the phone to Paton to come and see them and ERIC FAULKNER *(who had replaced DAVIE PATON)* and Tam and myself went to a gig in Dunbar. McKeown was nervous for the audition – he's no' that now! – and was jumpin' aboot the stage. He was good and we needed a front man, so he came in and we had a few more hits wi' Martin and Coulter.'

BAY CITY ROLLERS
A. LONGMUIR

115

By this time, the band had formally signed with Tam Paton as manager. Their first 'pro' wage was £7 a week, when Alan had been earning £20 to £40 as a plumber, and STUART WOOD had progressed from roadie to second guitar.

'In 1975, we began to do our own stuff. We had been involved with Peter Walsh at Starlight Agency and once we were stuck in Wales when we were double booked. I phoned up to explain the situation and say that we needed money. "Tough," he said, and Tam Paton's mother had to wire us the cash.

The operation in Prestonpans was really growing. We had 15 girls working and it was from the fan mail that the idea of using tartan came about. Woody ran about wi' skinheads and somebody had sent in a fashion idea of white gear with check trim. Eric Faulkner said, "That would look good in tartan."

Things were really big by the mid-Seventies. Sid Bernstein, who had promoted the BEATLES in America, came to Glasgow and couldn't believe it. We went over and had fantastic success. JOHN LENNON sent us a wee note wishin' us all the best, and one time in Canada we played in front of 65,000 people. It still cost money to get out of contracts, though (*£40,000 to Bernstein*), and generally we were ripped off.'

ALAN LONGMUIR finished with the band in 1976 and bought a smallholding near Dollar where, for a couple of years, he kept sheep and horses. He was asked to return and in 1978 they undertook a 13-week TV series in Los Angeles. He later starred in a small film, and a final Rollers album, entitled *Strangers In The Wind* was produced – although not without problems over which material should be included – and the entire operation collapsed soon afterwards.
In 1985/86 a hotel venture cost him his home and his marriage. At the time of writing he was preparing for a 'nostalgia' tour of the South of England, with ERIC FAULKNER and STUART WOOD.

116

CHAPTER THIRTEEN

BRUCE FINDLAY

'I thought managers were mugs . . .'

BRUCE FINDLAY *was a weel kent figure on the Scottish music scene in the Sixties and Seventies through his partnership in the Bruce's Record Shop chain. He briefly looked after an Edinburgh group,* CAFÉ JACQUES, *before starting an independent record label, and subsequently managing* SIMPLE MINDS *whom he steered from the Glasgow pubs to an international stage. By the time the relationship was dissolved, Simple Minds were Scotland's top-selling group throughout the world, and had made a major contribution to the eventual freedom of Nelson Mandela.*
Bruce now manages the SILENCERS.

'I was a big fan of trad jazz – I went to the balls in London – I liked dancing – and you could skip-jive to trad jazz. The Place was a trad jazz club and I used to go every week. Across the road at the Gamp, the Athenians played rock'n'roll. The pre-mods went there, and the beatnicky-types went to the Place. One Sunday night, the Place tried the ALEX HARVEY BIG SOUL BAND for an experiment *(1961)*. It was stunning. He had congas and percussion and the BLUES COUNCIL then became resident. LES HARVEY was the guitarist in this band and, very sadly, going back to Glasgow one night, they were involved in a car crash and the singer was killed.

I liked RAY CHARLES and MOSE ALLISON, and this was an introduction for the traddies to something new. There were lots of good Scottish musicians, but they gravitated towards London.

I tried to hitch-hike around the world in the early Sixties, and came back to work in my mother's record shop *(McDougall's)* in Falkirk. I tried pop promotion and wanted to bring the BEATLES to Falkirk. I phoned Brian Epstein and offered him £1,000 around the time of *From Me To You*, but the group had broken big by then. I went on to open Bruce's Record shops and, by 1974 I had become friendly with record companies, Island in particular. They said, "Why don't you form your own label, like Chrysalis or Bronze?"

I had been impressed by ALAN GORRIE and the VIKINGS in Falkirk – I gave them *Midnight Hour* one afternoon and they were playing it that night in the La Bamba club! – and I tried Island with one of their acetates *(DEEP PURPLE)* but they were turned down. I had also mentioned GERRY RAFFERTY and BILLY CONNOLLY to them, and they had taken the STRING BAND, but it was after they peaked.

By the mid-Seventies, I had promoted some Edinburgh Festival concerts – Island were prepared to offer me money and, for the first time in my life, I went out looking for a band like an A&R man. I saw this sort of soul-orientated group, CAFÉ JACQUES, in Edinburgh, but the record company maintained they were an album band and didn't want to invest. So I became their manager and got them a deal with CBS. They didn't go on to great things, but they recorded two albums and PHIL COLLINS was on one.

After a couple of years of management, I split. I thought managers were mugs – nobody likes them, and I wanted to be liked! I like to ingratiate myself and vibe people up! Then came punk rock.

I was 32 years of age and I thought I was too old, but punk rejuvenated me. I saw this band THE VALVES and you could start an indie label with hundreds of pounds rather than thousands, so I started ZOOM Records and The Valves got to number one in the independent charts with *For Adolphs Only*. SLIK then came to me and said, "Punk is gonna kill us, but we're good and that's the kind of music we like – not this Bill Martin teenybop stuff!" They had a great song – *We're Gonna Put You In The Picture* – power pop, and we put it out as *PVC2*. Another independent hit.

I liked hanging out and the bands didn't mind me coming backstage because I had record shops. I was determined to get involved in the creative side, though. I had seen JOHNNY AND THE SELF-ABUSERS somewhere *(Carlops, 1977?)* and the day their single came out on Chiswick, they split up. Half became SIMPLE MINDS and half, the CUBAN HEELS. JIM KERR came through in the spring of 1978 and played me a demo of five songs including *Chelsea Girl,* which sounded to me like a smash pop hit. But they also had this mesmeric underground sound, including violin. I thought they were the best thing I'd ever heard in my life and I was absolutely blown away. Also by Jim, who was 18. He was very skinny with a wee pudding-bowl haircut, mascara and pointed shoes. He wore black leather – gothic, like Hamlet, or something – and it impressed me; he was so young and hip.

I thought, "How can you walk down the streets of Glasgow and not get beaten up?" Punk had now been going for years and everyone was aggressive, but less so Jim, although he was tougher than he looked. I thought he was brave.

The night after, I had a young guy working for me – Brian Hogg – who went to see them and did a raving review for *Cripes,* our fanzine. He said, "It's the best thing I've ever seen" – so I was determined then.

I went through the following Sunday to the Mars Bar which was packed out, but they put me on the guest list. Jim says they were impressed that I wanted to see them! A wee pub – packed – with a sound man, and his sister doing the lights. They were art-rocky like ROXY MUSIC which was unfashionable in a way, because everyone else was into power-play. Jim had this balletic style, and the band were very powerful. I became their friend, their confidant.

I always liked a good song, but I also like the *sound* that music makes. SIMPLE MINDS were originally derivative, but there was a certain originality and I would like to have signed them to the record label although I didn't want to be their manager. At that time I had negotiated a distribution deal for Zoom with Arista records. I recognised that, with the punk explosion, the door would be open only for a little while before the Establishment took over. I knew that the only way to survive would be to get proper financial support but I was both right and wrong. I got a licence deal with Arista, but it was pathetic – £25,000 per year – and I had to deliver seven singles. It sounds like quite a lot of money but it's not much when you're talking about a record company.

I immediately saw Simple Minds as an album band. They had enough material and although there were lots of influences, they didn't sound like the SEX PISTOLS, which every other band did. They hadn't played outside Scotland and didn't want to go to London for, say, showcase gigs at the Hope and Anchor or the Nashville. They had a little bit of record company interest but they were very cautious – still are – about who they might sign to. They said, "We'd really like to sign to an independent, but we're not daft" – these were 18-year-old kids – "We need the power of a major because we want to buy a PA, lights, put ourselves on wages." So I became their "manager in waiting", driving them to all the gigs.

Finally, after two or three record companies had come up here, Arista said, "Why don't you sign them to Zoom? We'll give you the money and do a second Zoom deal exclusive to Simple Minds." So they got the independent deal with the clout of the major, although I let the record company thing slip because they needed a manager. I didn't sign any more bands after that, and Arista didn't really capitalise on the independent Scottish nature of the label.

We then drew up a list of producers. John Leckie came up to see them in Dundee, loved them, and we went into the studio the next day. The album *Life In A Day* was recorded in four weeks in 1978, and released early in 1979. We charted before we had played in England!, and thank God, because the first gig in London, supporting MAGAZINE, was a disaster. It was a good tour but a lot of things went wrong in London. Plugs pulled etc.

There was never any Scottish nationalism – when the band did their first interviews, they were written up phonetically, and they hated it. They wanted to be an international band – not part of any "new, young Scotland" or any of that. I hate

119

nationalism, but I'm very Scottish. I'm as patriotic as they come, and I'm for retention of culture.

Anyway, the first album charted and I got them a *Whistle Test*. We had a good plan: we knew we wouldn't be able to rely on Britain as their music was a bit different, so we got a good agent right away and started to tour prolifically around Europe and the UK. When people bumped into us in Germany, word would come back that we were huge over there – although we were only playing to a few hundred people.

Our first Top 20 hit was actually in Canada – *Love Song* – and our first gold album was in Australia. A few Scots would turn out, but we didn't make it because we were Scots. We were perceived as a European-sounding band, and didn't rest on our laurels. It was onwards and upwards – progressive rock in the true sense – and besides experimenting, they had a phenomenal work record. I don't know of any band that's played as many gigs as SIMPLE MINDS *(NAZARETH?)*. We did 250 gigs, year in and year out. The band made five albums in three years and did 700 gigs. There were casualties, although nothing too serious, and actually I'm about to become a casualty myself! It's time for a fresh challenge, so myself and the band are splitting up.

However, the real breakthrough came when we left Arista for Virgin. They did a good job on the double album and in 1985 we were asked to do a song for a

Opposite: SIMPLE MINDS ROCK GARDEN

121

film sound-track, which made a US number one. Our bank was brilliant, although banks don't normally help rock bands. I'd put them on wages right away and I always prided myself on the way the books were kept – we always paid bills and taxes. *New Gold Dream* finally wiped out the debt which had reached £4-500,000, but the business is like a swingometer. Two per cent one way is high loss, two per cent the other, big profit, although it wasn't until 1987 that we began to see real money, when the *Once Upon A Time* album sold three million.'

NELSON MANDELA

'Jerry Dammers approached Jim in 1988 to do an anti-apartheid gig, but we wanted something more focused, something special. The anniversary – 70th birthday and 25 years in jail – was the thing so, in a sense, Jim was the prime mover. Really, of course, it is the efforts of Tutu and Bishop Trevor Huddleston which have achieved most and the hard-working guys in the anti-apartheid movement – they work hard and the Press don't give a shit. Pop stars and film stars, however, they bring people. A billion in the case of Mandela. Politicians love pop stars.'

BRUCE FINDLAY
APPLAUSE MAGAZINE

CHAPTER FOURTEEN

KENNY HYSLOP

'If you want to be a drummer, get out of this house'

KENNY HYSLOP has probably had more major recording deals than any other Scottish-based musician.

'I was born in Helensburgh in 1951. My father had a draper's shop in the town and wanted me to go into the family business. My head was full of drumming, though, ever since I had seen the SHADOWS doing *Apache*. I drove my parents crazy playin' with knittin' needles on chairs and my knuckles on the table. I built up a drum kit through various presents and Christmas monies and we had a school band at Helensburgh Academy – THE OTHERS – with Jim Yule, later of pre-Cado Belle group UP, and NEW CELESTE.

I had no interest in school and failed all my exams as a result. I just wanted to carry on drumming, and my father said, "If you want to be a drummer, get out of this house."

So, by this time I was in another band called PRAM, a three-piece with GERRY EADIE and RAYMOND O'DONNELL, and we moved up to Glasgow and shared a flat together. I was about 18 and we did youth clubs, school dances, then places like Sgt Peppers, Picasso, Burns Howff, the Watermill and the Bundoran club which was in Sauchiehall Street above the Third Eye. When Pram split up I joined the BEINGS with Davie Kirkwood and DOUGIE THOMPSON *(later of SUPERTRAMP)* for they were very active and had a six-wheel transit which was hip! After that I had six weeks with NORTHWIND, but they were all smokin' and too laid back, so I had to get away, and in 1973 I auditioned for SALVATION. This was a group built around the McGinlay brothers, Jim and Kevin, and their manager Eddie Tobin was looking for a new line-up to play the discos around town. MIDGE URE and I were asked to join. Midge had been in a band from Rutherglen called STUMBLE, and BILLY MacISAAC became the keyboard player.

At first, Kevin stayed on as singer and it was the days of glam rock *(1974/75)* so he used to change costume at one point, and Midge would do a couple of songs on his own. He was lovin' it, but it must be said that he was one of the keenest and hardworkin' people I've played with. Very ambitious and dedicated. Anyway,

Kevin began to get a bit overshadowed and left, and at that point we changed to SLIK. Frank Lynch came in as manager with his partner, Max Langdon, and they were building an empire. They were the first to get licences after ten for discos like the Savoy, Electric Garden, and Maestros *(formerly Maryland)* and later they had the Apollo and Clouds.

We only had two or three original songs at this time . . . we were like a mobile disco, and we wanted to get away from that but nobody in London thought our own stuff was commercial enough. So they sold us to Bill Martin and Phil Coulter and our first single was a number one *(Forever And Ever, 1976)*. They also wrote for the BAY CITY ROLLERS, who were also on Bell Records. We had a great year out of it, although we didn't see much in the way of royalties. We were just on wages – it was take it or leave it – and we took it, thinkin' it would benefit our individual careers in the long run. Also, we were right on the brink of punk rock, and the only image band to survive that was GARY GLITTER.

So we tried to go New Wave – changed our hair styles and started writin' angry songs – and we did a single as *PVC2* for Bruce Findlay's Zoom label. But the bigger companies wouldn't accept the change. Midge got an offer from RICH KIDS *(Glen Matlock's offshoot from the SEX PISTOLS)* and we got another singer/guitarist – WILLIE GARDNER from MODERN MAN who was great . . . Glasgow's ELVIS COSTELLO. Plus BILLY MacISAAC, and RUSSELL WEBB who had been at university – the next step was the ZONES.

We did mostly our own songs – it was the time of the Mars Bar and the Saints and Sinners which we played with JOHNNY AND THE SELF ABUSERS – and we got a deal with Arista. It fell apart at a crucial stage, however . . . we were waiting to do our biggest London gig, and Willie had to go back to Glasgow . . . and I became a bit disillusioned. Russell and myself at one point got a call from RICKY JOBSON to play on a SKIDS single, but when we went up to Inverness to do it, STUART ADAMSON was there but Jobson wasn't. They didn't get on, and it was the same sketch at the mix. When I was hasslin' to get my money Stuart and Simon Draper *(Virgin)* said if I stayed with the band I'd get paid! I said, "What?" There was no incentive when they didn't get on, although I did eventually get paid, and I suppose I also missed the chance to join BIG COUNTRY. Russell later worked with Jobson in the ARMOURY SHOW.

I was sick of bands then, and took a year out workin' as a DJ, to keep in touch with the music. It was the time of POSTCARD in Glasgow, but I was more interested in what was happening in London at the time. The New Romantics.

Then I got the SIMPLE MINDS thing, replacing BRIAN McGHEE. They had just

finished *Sons and Fascination* and it was just a case of me learning the beats. They were also like Midge ... hard-working, keen to rehearse, write and tour. I did a world tour in 1981 ... Australia, America, Europe and it was a great experience. They were very much in debt, but the record company believed that hard touring would eventually get them off the ground. So the wages weren't great, although I was earning more than the band.

Then we came back to rehearse *New Gold Dream*, I was in love with this New York dance track and was playin' it all the time on my walkman. JIM KERR asked me what it was and I blasted it out. Next thing we were jammin' on it and he wrote *Promised You a Miracle*. It gave them their first hit, but ... going back ... I had been jammin' with BOBBY PATERSON in Glasgow and CHRIS MORGAN who was a character who went to the clubs. Island Records became interested in what we were doin' and we were about to do an albums deal because my Minds' contract was at an end. Now, *Promised You A Miracle* was sounding good and their management said, "If you leave, you just get wages." I thought it was terrible, I should have my fifth anyway. So that sickened me and I took my ideas to Island. I also started sending tapes to myself after that. Cheapest form of copyright.

With SET THE TONE we were well set up, but Chris Morgan blew it. He thought he could run around Island Records drunk, in 1982, screaming into office doorways.

SET THE TONE with
CHRIS BLACKWELL
(centre) ROCK GARDEN

He was like a frustrated punk, and Chris Blackwell said, "You'll need to find a new singer, or you're off the label." We couldn't get anybody in time, so that was that. We just did one album, but we saw some cash and good equipment. I had been influenced by the heavier black stuff that was comin' out of America. The dirty synth bass sounds and rock drumbeat, like early PRINCE stuff. FRANKIE GOES TO HOLLYWOOD did the same thing, but with better production.

Then it was a natural progression to the ONE O'CLOCK GANG. LAURIE CUFFE from the CUBAN HEELS, FRANK O'HARE and STEVIE DOYLE. We also had the guy who managed SET THE TONE in charge of the money, and he took us to the cleaners as well. The thing ended in disarray, with VAT people impounding the gear, after we had got another deal with Arista.

My *musical* problem appears to have been that I've always experimented with stuff, trying to get something innovative off the ground as opposed to copyin' trends . . . crossing styles, and I don't know if that's a fault or not.

Anyway, in 1985, I went down for Live Aid although I couldn't get a ticket and watched it on the telly with Max Langdon. Next day I went over to Midge's house, and ended up doing his solo tour with ZAL CLEMINSON – who must be the best guitarist I've every worked with. Another wee jaunt round the world.

Maybe I "still haven't found what I'm looking for", but if it's good, I'll be into it.'

126

CHAPTER FIFTEEN

BARRY WRIGHT

'Every generation has a right to its own music'

If Tin Pan Alley ever really existed, then one of its most famous structures was surely New York's Brill Building, an office block at 1619 Broadway where, in the late Fifties, Al Nevins and Don Kirshner had established a 'song factory' whose work-force included LIEBER AND STOLLER, NEIL SEDAKA, GERRY GOFFIN and CAROLE KING. In the late 1980s the concept of collective interest suddenly had an effect on Scotland's rapidly-developing music scene.

By the summer of 1988, Regular Music – Scotland's leading popular music promotions company – had outgrown its premises at Castlecliff in Edinburgh and were looking for a new home. It transpired that Rock Steady, the firm which supplied stewards for the regular concerts, were virtually the sole occupants of an office block adjacent to the Playhouse Theatre and, having accommodated the rock impresarios in its spacious attic, Greenside House was on its way to becoming a nerve-centre of the Scottish music business. Soon there were ticket agents, graphic designers, management companies and a Press Office, something which hitherto had never existed in Scottish music.

   Regular is one of Scotland's principal pop music success stories. Says director, Barry Wright:

'I came from Dunfermline originally and was more interested in folk music when I was younger. I used to hang about the Howff club. I went to Edinburgh University late – in 1968 – and was more interested in student politics and newspaper publishing. I put on some charity gigs and Pete Irvine *(fellow director, Regular)* had promoted some stuff at the El Dorado in Leith. Around 1976, I was living out in Humbie and I met a guy who had run into FRANKIE MILLER in London and wanted to put on a show in Scotland. We promoted him at Edinburgh Tiffany's and Glasgow City Hall and made £300. I thought I could do it and make a living. I pottered away on my own for a year then did some gigs at the 1977 Edinburgh Festival.

   Pete joined me the following year, and we began to expand. In 1979 we decided to do an outdoor show at Ingliston, but despite the quality of the bill – VAN MORRISON, TALKING HEADS, THE UNDERTONES, CHIEFTAINS and others – we misjudged it. There was no habit of our outdoor shows in Scotland and we got it wrong by

BARRY WRIGHT
B. WRIGHT

deciding to put on a *show* instead of having the act first. We lost £120,000, our houses were on the line, and we spent the next couple of years changing from being amateur to being professional. When we woke up two or three years later, we had moved from 100 shows per year to 250.

We were the ones who persuaded English bands and others to come to Scotland *regularly*. Previously the gigs had been sporadic. When we started, ten per cent of tour dates were in Scotland. We think that has now doubled. The big tours have contracted, but the groups are still doing two, three, four gigs in Scotland. Also, more Scottish kids are going to gigs and more Scottish bands are coming through. In Ireland, where there is a very young population, more people go to live music than in any other European country.

I think that the generations since the last war have learned their identity, their politics, fashion etc, through music. Sometimes it comes from the record companies and sometimes from the streets. We became more interested again after punk, and we grew with SIMPLE MINDS. We don't put on music we consider to be "product", or heavy metal, or things we don't understand but, otherwise, it's a pretty eclectic mix, and every generation has a right to its own music; so if properly organised, why not?

You can't make huge profits. The days of 50/50 deals are over and the VAT man now takes more than the promoter. Normally the band will get 85 per cent of whatever is left after expenses, but this is only on 40 to 50 per cent of the gross, so we are only on five to seven per cent.

We have tried to convince the SDA *(Scottish Development Agency)* of directions they should go in, since they told us we are doing 40 per cent of the live promoting in Scotland, but they appear to have lots of money for surveys and none for capital projects. We've simply decided on a Hadrian's Wall Policy – if it comes over the wall, go for it! It means we can get to a show every day, and I don't have to spend six months away from home every year.

When we were young, anyone who got chart success immediately went for London management. SIMPLE MINDS were one of the first who didn't do this, and succeeded, and now we have a little community here which recognises itself as Scottish. Once you're seen to survive, you begin to attract others – accountants, lawyers, insurance, studios, plus graphics, press management companies, TV production companies, security and so forth. And we're seeing the beginnings of professional PA and lighting companies.

We're just enablers. We don't have to love everything but, if we believe something to be honest, we give it space.'

CHAPTER SIXTEEN

EDWYN COLLINS

'It seemed that anything was possible'

EDWYN COLLINS was born in Edinburgh in 1959. Both his parents were art students, and his maternal grandfather – Stewart MacIntosh – was a well-known educationalist who helped pioneer comprehensive education in Scotland; he was also a Scottish rugby internationalist. In 1965, Edwyn's father moved to Dundee to take up a lecturing post at Duncan of Jordanstone College of Art, and Edwyn was enrolled at the Demonstration School, a progressive liberal teaching establishment attached to Dundee's College of Education. ALAN RANKINE of the ASSOCIATES was also a pupil. He then moved to Morgan Academy.

'I had had violin lessons, but had lost interest although my parents bought records and one of my uncles played a nylon string guitar. At 13 or 14 I bought *Aladdin Sane*, and there was talk of people getting groups together. One was a heavy rock group called ONYX, and I wanted to join them. I really wanted to play saxophone, but whereas other parents bought kids instruments, mine didn't want to encourage me in that direction. I had a ukulele, though, and I offered to put a pick-up on it. But it seemed that they didn't need an electric ukulele player! Actually, I was also very slight at this time, and doubt if I had reached puberty. The others were more mature and popular with girls, and I think they thought I'd be an embarrassment. They never did any gigs, of course, they just rehearsed in people's houses.

My folks wanted me to go to university, although I was good at art and wanted to go to art college. Anyway, they split up when I was 15, and I went to Glasgow with my mother and younger sister. Because she had left art school to have me, my mother had no qualifications, and she went to work with British Steel as a clerk in Govan. We stayed with relatives at first, in Bearsden, then got a house in Courthill.

At Bearsden Academy, I was slagged to bits for wearing what was high fashion in Dundee – desert boots and flared trousers with turn-ups. Also DAVID BOWIE/ROD STEWART haircuts were *de rigueur* at Bearsden and they thought I had a BRIAN JONES haircut. I suppose even then I was quite interested in Sixties music. They said, "Look at the gallus hush puppies!" I didn't even know what they meant, and as for my Dundonian words, they'd find them hilarious.

I found it hard to make friends initially, and the place quite intimidating, although RODDY FRAME says he finds East Coast people more violent. Most of the Bearsden kids were academic and cliquey, and I had decided that I wasn't really for that. They liked the EAGLES and PETER FRAMPTON, whereas I was into LOU REED and the VELVET UNDERGROUND. I was also going to the Barras and buying old TROGGS singles. I liked the sound of them because they were really crude. Other kids had resigned themselves to the scrapheap, and some idolised the Drumchapel gangs.

In 1975, there were articles in the papers on the New York groups, TELEVISION, BLONDIE and the NEW YORK DOLLS – and I thought they were right up my street. I had this romantic notion of myself as the alienated misfit, and in Listen Records *(Glasgow, run by the MacNaughton Brothers of Arran and Carioca fame)* I had found this BUDDY HOLLY button badge. A guy in the year below me at school – Stephen Daly – asked me where I'd got it and said he was forming a punk group with another pupil in the fifth year – James Kirk – called the MACHETÉS. By this time I had pawned my stamp album for a Burns Nu-Sonic guitar. It was only £20 but my mother couldn't afford it and again, didn't really want to encourage me. I had also got a WEM Dominator amp – it was more kitsch, really – James Kirk had got a guitar through a catalogue and, although Stephen Daly was originally the singer, he had now become the drummer. Another guy, Alan Duncan, had a bass, so we formed a group called the NU SONICS.

Around 1977, there was a group called the HOT CITY COWBOYS who did covers and there was a gig at the Bearsden Burgh Hall where they were supported by a hard core punk group called the SHOCK. This was run by a guy called FRANK RAFFERTY who was intelligent but crazy and he had his own gang called the Wessy Rats. Frank would come to the school and talk to James, Stephen and me about punk, and so I went to the gig. Now, what the sociologists forget is that punk was not a working-class phenomenon, but something engineered by these art students, Bernard Rhodes and Malcolm MacLaren, who were into Dada, and at first, the real "proles" hated it. So we had straight trousers on that night, and were beaten up by a Drumchapel gang, the Drum Derry. We were taken to hospital and my friend got 17 stitches in his head. That's why I always make jokes about fighting the punk rock wars!

The next thing was the WHITE RIOT tour at the Playhouse in Edinburgh. We went through in the afternoon and helped them in with their gear. James and Stephen had primarily gone to see the CLASH, but the most appealing groups to me were the SUBWAY SECT and the SLITS. I didn't take the politics too seriously, especially as it had been revealed that JOE STRUMMER had been to Westminster Public School, but the other groups could hardly play at all, and they also had really cheap equipment like we had. It seemed that anything was possible. This could be your entrée into music.

By late 1977, I had left school and was on the dole. We used to go to gigs at the Silver Thread in Paisley, run by a guy called Disco Harry and featuring the BUZZCOCKS, GENERATION X . . . There was also this guy called Arthur Haggerty who was a kind of punk entrepreneur and ran the buses to the Paisley gigs. He worked at Bruce's Records and Stephen worked at Listen, in the basement, and we got our first gig through Arthur. Punk was infiltrating all the soul clubs by now, straight trousers, skinny ties, and we would sometimes go to Shuffles for a laugh, but this gig was at Satellite City, above the Apollo. There was STEEL PULSE, THE BACKSTABBERS *(later JAMES KING AND LONE WOLVES)*, JOHNNY AND THE SELF-ABUSERS *(later SIMPLE MINDS)* and the NU SONICS. I had switched to lead vocals, and Stephen Daly had a drum kit which he got in the Barras for 40 quid and had only been playing for four weeks!

We liked the BACKSTABBERS *(vocalist, Rev Volting)* who had a kind of frenetic craziness, but SIMPLE MINDS we thought of as "pub" or "art rock", and not authentic. They were just adapting other people's ideas – JONATHAN RICHMOND, the CLASH, ROXY MUSIC, NICO – and we thought of them as cabaret. We were completely disdainful of them, because we had written all our own material and it was precocious lyrically, and not moronic, like JOHNNY AND THE SELF-ABUSERS. We were very serious about punk and rock'n'roll and demanded commitment from people who were performing. Whatever you thought about groups at that time, they were completely committed and when people debased this we would be upset.

By 1978, however, it had degenerated into the "Oi" groups – SHAM 69 and the UK SUBS – who were racist and unthinking . . . football hooligans. I don't mean that to sound élitist or snobby, but we wanted to dissociate ourselves from that kind of thing. We thought ORANGE JUICE was a name that would infuriate other punks and get us a bit of interest. It was absurd in the context of punk.

ALAN HORNE was a student from Saltcoats who was doing botany at Glasgow University. He had been at the Satellite City gig, thought we were camp and funny, and produced a fanzine called *Swankers* in which he enthused about the BACKSTABBERS and NU SONICS. He had also met Stephen at Listen and liked the few crude demos we had made *(1979)*. He had this huge trunk. He had gone round record auctions and got all the Stax and Atlantic singles and stuff on Elektra, like the DOORS and LOVE. If you wanted to check up on things, you'd go to Alan's box . . . it was like a musical education. The group which was inspiring me at that time from Alan's box was the BYRDS . . . not a dissimilar sound to the VELVET UNDERGROUND . . . jangly guitars. When we welded this on to the punk rhythm section, Alan thought it sounded completely fresh and was inspired to want to make a record.

The bass player by this time was DAVID McCLYMONT. We had met at Printing College, although I had dropped out ... but to make a commitment to music seemed flaky – a huge step – and it was impossible to explain punk to my mother or uncle, those who were concerned about my career. I actually wanted to be an illustrator ... I had a good portfolio of wildlife illustration, and I got a job with Glasgow's Parks Department, designing leaflets for Nature Trails. David also worked there.

Anyway, Alan came up to the office and said, "My favourite song of yours is *Falling and Laughing*," which I had written when I was 17. We recorded it at John McLarty's eight-track "wardrobe" in Paisley and it was the first single on the Postcard record label *(February 1980)*. We also had a live flexi-disc of a song called *Felicity* so it went into the package, together with one of four postcards. MALCOLM ROSS *(of TV ART, later JOSEF K)* helped with the production and we had vague ideas of a label roster, but obviously couldn't afford one at that stage.

A thousand singles were made. David and I paid half from our wages at the Parks Department, Alan Horne's parents paid the other half, and it cost something like £500 in total. It was single of the week in *Melody Maker* and *Smash Hits*, and got a good review in *Sounds*, which attracted the attention of Geoff Travis at Rough Trade. He took 300 copies, Small Wonder got 100, Red Rhino 100, a hundred to journalists ... we got our money back almost straight away. Geoff Travis also indicated that if the next single was of the same standard he would be interested in doing a manufacture and distribution deal. We thought we were set up.

TV ART had also put out a single, partly financed by Stephen Daly, and it had received no attention. Alan said if they would change their name to JOSEF K, he would manage them and put out the next single. So, with the money we got from *Falling and Laughing*, we went to Castle Sound Studios near Edinburgh which was fantastic. We recorded the next ORANGE JUICE A&B side in the morning and JOSEF K did theirs in the afternoon. It came out in the August *(1980)*. By this time we were getting a fair bit of attention in Scotland, but when Alan and I went to London, Travis said *Blue Boy (ORANGE JUICE)* and *Radio Drill Time (JOSEF K)* fell into no man's land. They were neither independent post-punk nor sophisticated enough for radio play. Alan was devastated and furious. He went into a kind of trance and when we stormed out of the shop he was almost run over! I said "Look, it's no problem ... we just try the majors ..." "Aye, that's right," he said "Betray me! Betray me!"

His parents gave him the money to press 2,000 copies of each new single, and we hand-coloured them with fluorescent pens. We sent out review copies and

Dave McCulloch and Paul Morley (*Sounds and NME respectively*) each gave us two-page spreads while Billy Sloan did something in *Record Mirror*. All on the same day! So we went back to Rough Trade and, lo and behold, Geoff Travis had had a very dramatic change of heart! We got a very good percentage deal and the singles went on to sell around 10,000 copies each. We then did a single with an Australian group, the GO-BETWEENS, and finally we saw AZTEC CAMERA at the Bungalow Bar in Paisley. Roddy was just 16 and the group sounded like LOVE. So we had our roster, but it wasn't like a business. We just wanted to get on with it. I mean, initially, the music itself had been secondary – we just wanted to get up on stage – although by now, production was becoming more important.

By 1981, when the last ORANGE JUICE single on Postcard came out, we were being investigated by the dole, so we had to go on to wages – £20 a week, and it wasn't much to live on. Also, as far as gigs went, Glasgow remained a closed shop . . . Richard Park at Clyde was quite supportive, but the City Stewards people, George Duffin and the guy in the Third Eye . . . they said, "Go away and learn to sing and play!" And whereas Geoff Travis had a *volte-face,* these guys continued to resent us. The Regular people were more accommodating. Pete and Barry liked us and we did the Nightclub beside the Playhouse. By this time, ORANGE JUICE were selling 20,000 singles and JOSEF K's album did 12,000 or something. We had also always had interest from the majors but when people phoned up, Alan would tell them to fuck off! The majors didn't know how to market the groups . . . they couldn't assimilate the punk aesthetic.

Rough Trade financed the first ORANGE JUICE album, *You Can't Hide Your Love Forever,* but Stephen wasn't happy with Alan and Postcard and the producer, Adam Kidron, wanted to try the majors. We signed a tape-lease deal with Polydor which gave us control over marketing, packaging and production.

Polydor should have capitalised on our grass-roots following, but they saw us as a left-field group who could pull a crowd. They knew something was happening but they didn't know why. On the singles, the sales were there but not in the chart shops, and the group just split up. JOSEF K had also split up and I invited MALCOLM ROSS into the group, but he and DAVID McCLYMONT then proceeded to force my hand into splitting from James and Stephen. ZEKE MANYIKA (*from Zimbabwe via Glasgow*) then came in on drums and in 1982 we did the *Rip It Up* album. It was the year of "new pop" and the first record to feature the Roland bass sound. The riff came from Nile Rodgers.

Texas Fever was the second-last album and commercial suicide. Denis Bovell produced it and by the time we did *The Orange Juice* album, there was only Denis,

Zeke and myself. By then Polydor had lost interest and wanted to concentrate on Zeke's world music demos. In 1986 I did two nights at the Bloomsbury Theatre with a new set of songs. It got a great reaction from the music press, but apparently I had a reputation for being dogmatic and opinionated. Grace *(Maxwell)* had been managing ORANGE JUICE, then I did it myself, then we tried another guy, but although he had connections, he was clueless as far as I was concerned, so Grace and I began to consider financing something ourselves.

In 1989 I got a phone-call asking if I'd like to check out White House Studios in Cologne. ORANGE JUICE had apparently influenced some German bands and they wanted us to record there. The studio then licensed what we recorded there to Demon *(Elvis Costello and Jake Riviera),* and as *Hope And Despair,* it sold around 35,000 copies. Now we've done another one at Robin Miller's Powerplant – *Hellbent On Compromise* – so I'm quite happy now. We've also done some live stuff in Austria and Germany.

Scottish music: I don't like cosmetic Scottish things, or the pomp of Scottish music. I like atmospheres. Also, I don't think people really want world music. Rock'n'roll is world music, the music of poor immigrants – and that's not theory, it's fact.

Scots have got to shake off that "just be ordinary in your life" attitude. We genuinely believed with Postcard that our music was better than the London groups. And I was never really that interested in Burns. I'd read Scott Fitzgerald, or something, although I am interested in the pentatonic scale. I realised that when I stopped writing intuitively and started analysing what it was I liked about music. Now I maybe try to write a five-note melody instead of something from the European tradition.

I think if you believe in something, the conviction comes across. A lot of the new bands get their sensibilities from Wrangler and Levi ads. Also, I'm probably from the last generation of musicians with any kind of techno fear! But at least nowadays I'm more relaxed about my voice. I can take it or leave it.'

EDWYN COLLINS
GRACE MAXWELL

DEACON BLUE
CBS RECORDS

SUGAR SUGAR
ROCK GARDEN

136

GILLIAN MAXWELL
GILLIAN MAXWELL

CHAPTER SEVENTEEN

GILLIAN MAXWELL

'We were left with the champagne bottles and the train tickets home'

GILLIAN MAXWELL is a Director of DEACON BLUE'S management company and runs its Scottish office in Glasgow.

'I was born in Glasgow in 1956. I went to Jordanhill school, primary and secondary, although I didn't want to do a sixth year at school and, instead, went to Langside College for extra 'A' levels. My family lived in the West End, I have a brother and sister, and I got a place at Glasgow University.

There was no music in the family although my father liked "real" boogie woogie – NEVILLE DICKIE – and I took classical piano lessons for six or seven years. My teacher wanted to teach classics only, however, and I was getting interested in other things . . . T REX and the like.

My degree was in Moral Philosophy. It attracted me because there were no rights and wrongs as in science. It was logical thought, debate and points of view. You had to learn how to present an argument and that has been useful to me.

After a year or so, I began to get involved in running the QM Student Union. I was on the Social Committee for a couple of months then became Social Convenor and, ultimately, Entertainments Convenor. Of course, my studies went to pot that year. A number of my contemporaries – Grace Maxwell who now manages EDWYN COLLINS and Kirsty MacNeill who wrote for the *NME* – also went on to work in the music business.

After university, I bombarded the BBC with letters and eventually got a clerking job with the film unit. I had a lot of enthusiasm at first and made contact with people like Bill Forsyth and Charlie Gormley who were forever trying to scrounge unused film *(1979)*. I stuck it for two years but couldn't get into the areas I wanted to – features, or music and arts. In fact, I had a terrible time at the BBC simply because there was a level above which women were not allowed to rise. They went sideways and the furthest most got was the level of Production Assistant where they stayed for 20 years. Coming out of university with a lot of enthusiasm and feeling I had a mark to make, I very quickly became disillusioned at not even getting a chance. So I left.

Musically, things were quite interesting at this time. At school, I wasn't aware of local bands or gigs apart from the Maryland. When we got to the Students Union, however, I began to notice support bands and wanted to take chances with people like CADO BELLE, CHOW PARROT, CHICO, CROPPA and CAFÉ JACQUES. I went out on a limb on occasion and some of these bands did quite well. If Cado Belle, for example, had been around in the Eighties, they would definitely have been a major group. They were the first band I remember being actively involved with who seemed to be going somewhere and it was hugely exciting.

I also did some promoting after university with Mark Goldinger. We borrowed some money and had good ideas, but no business knowledge at that time. We did GENERATION X *(Billy Idol)* and the STEVE GIBBONS BAND but they were financial disasters.

When I was at the BBC, I was still interested in music but it was the post-punk thing and I felt too old for it. When I left, I knew I wanted to go into the music business, but Glasgow had gone a bit quiet and the Mars Bar was the only place to see anyone.

I was unemployed for some considerable time, just floating around doing bits and pieces, and some friends – JIM McNULTY, GRAHAM KELLING and ROBBIE ROSS – formed a band called ON A CLEAR DAY . . . very avant-garde, and I was the manager. Jim was interested in stuff like SYLVESTER and the gay disco scene and they had a following, but began to diverge musically and he went on to SUGAR SUGAR whilst Graham began to play with ALAN McCUSKER THOMSON in the PAINTED WORD *(1984)*.

For me, it seemed there was a choice . . . either you resigned yourself to earning money in a job which offered no opportunities or you had to be prepared to live on no money and go for it. We went without everything . . .

PAINTED WORD was the biggest stab we had at getting something happening, but they were a 12-piece band with strings, and playing in places like the Fixx was a nightmare. I got them a deal with Electra UK – A&R activity was really picking up in Glasgow around this time *(1985)* – but the day we were due to sign, we were in London, sitting in the office of our lawyer, John Kennedy, and a call came through from the States that Electra UK was to be closed and merged with WEA. SIMPLY RED, who had just signed with Electra UK, were picked up by WEA, but we were left with the champagne bottles and the train tickets home . . .

Everybody was very depressed by this experience but we had to try and pick up the pieces. We continued to gig – DOUGIE VIPOND was the drummer occasionally and JIM PRIME the keyboard player – and at my thirtieth birthday party at the Fixx, someone brought along RICKY ROSS *(February 1986)*. He had come to Glasgow from Dundee where he had done a B.Ed., and was teaching English and Drama. Dougie and Jim had met him and were looking for help in organising gigs. Ricky already had a publishing deal with ATV Music but it was contingent upon there being a band and his first band, WOZA, had not worked out. I heard his demos and saw him sing at Panama Jax – I was very impressed – so I agreed to help out, in addition to the work I was doing with the PAINTED WORD.

It seemed that most of the musicians I was mixing with at this time had not gone into music straight from school as with earlier generations. A lot had come from further education. Perhaps those who went straight from school were more attracted to the punk thing.

Anyway, Graham and Ewen *(Vernal)* then joined DEACON BLUE and subsequently, LORRAINE MacINTOSH. She was from Ayrshire and had been doing teacher training at Jordanhill. She was involved with Andy Thornton's early bands – BIG SUR and RATTLING CAGE – singing backup, and Ricky asked her to join. I had seen her at a pub soundcheck by chance and she really struck me immediately. When Ricky mentioned her name I was all for it.

They did some demos on Ricky's 8-track and I began to get some A&R money from my contacts to do 24-track demos, at Park Lane Studios. These were then circulated round the majors and Gordon Charlton from CBS picked up on them, as did Peter Felstead who had a lot of record company experience in London. He subsequently became manager, because the group needed top-flight management and I still had commitments with PAINTED WORD. So it then became a many-pronged attack upon the record companies, from Peter, myself and Sally Perryman of ATV Music.

Meanwhile, we were gigging around Scotland and there was pick-up right away. The Fixx, Fat Sam's, the Venue in Edinburgh . . . Scotland was really jumping at this time and it was sometimes hard to actually get gigs. BIG DISH were playing, as were WET WET WET and there was talk of this singer about to leave university *(PAT KANE)*. We also got help from various journalists – Billy Sloan, Tom Morton, John Dingwall, John Williamson, Andrea Miller . . . so we didn't have to flood the record companies with demos. They read about the groups in the music press and A&R men were arriving in their hordes.

Everybody at that time was keen to stay in Scotland and not move to London. We had management in London but our ethic has always been to keep things as Scottish as possible. On tours, for example, which have been my responsibility for the last four or five years, I would automatically take on a Scottish crew and use

Scottish companies where possible. Re-investment, if you like, and, of course, I think what Elliot Davis and Alan MacNeill have done with their studios is amazing. I applaud them for it – it's a good way to bring others through.

For the first three years we were touring Britain constantly and then Europe. We did the college and club circuits over and over again until we began to see results. Each time we went back to places we would try to go into a bigger venue, and I'm convinced that that was what worked for us – although sometimes records had to be re-released before we actually got hits.

I've now given up tour management because I've had no social or family life for five years and David, who also works with the DEACON BLUE organisation, and myself have been trying to find the time to get married for the last three years.

The life is very punishing . . . months and months on end, 18 to 20 hours a day, first up and last to bed. Switched-on at all times . . . no time for sight-seeing because you've got calls to make or interviews to arrange. It's hugely enjoyable but, after five years . . . . So now I've re-arranged my responsibilities with Peter and for the last six months have been overseeing videos, press and graphics – much of which is done in Scotland.

As far as I'm aware, there are four female tour managers at my level but I never cease to be amazed at the difficulty of finding female crew members. When we started, my brother and I were the DEACON BLUE crew. On the last tour there were 55 people, only four of whom were women. I can't put my finger on why women are not coming forward. I mean, you rarely need an electronics degree, and especially not in my position.

Sometimes I get letters after tours from girls and I try to encourage them. All you need is patience and a cool head . . . and at times you have to have a mouth . . . but I haven't encountered too much hostility. If you're seen to be doing the job well, people will have respect for you.

On the record company side and with lawyers and accountants, things are a bit different. There are certain attitudes which run right through these companies, regarding women. Having said that, we don't have enough lawyers or accountants in Scotland with music business experience and that's what we need . . . along with proper record companies. There has been talk of the majors coming to Glasgow or Edinburgh, but it hasn't happened yet.

However, we do have specialised stage services, set designers and artists, transport people and journalists. Also, there are rehearsal rooms and studios so the situation in Scotland will sustain itself.'

CHAPTER EIGHTEEN

PAT KANE

'. . . *that politicisation of the atmosphere linked in with a parallel development towards cultural autonomy*'

PAT KANE was born in 1964 and grew up in Coatbridge. Both sets of grandparents were native Irish and his father was a white-collar railway worker. A family achievement which is proudly remembered is that his grandfather was the first Catholic head of Coatbridge Bowling Club.

HUE & CRY CIRCA RECORDS

In the late summer of 1983, I was approached by two friends, Stephen Conway and Larry Spears, who were considering funding a single for two young Lanarkshire song-writers – Bill Docherty and Pierrot Jamieson – and their band, RODEO. They wanted me to assist with the production. It was a good song which I still remember – but the lead voice was not terribly strong and I suggested they look for a singer. When the next demo arrived, the voice exceeded my wildest expectations. It belonged to a 19-year-old, Pat Kane from Coatbridge, and the quality was that of a young GEORGE BENSON. In the studio I was not disappointed – he virtually did the thing in one take and any requested changes had to be justified to him – and, so enthusiastic was I, I volunteered to use some of my own contacts in London to try to arrange a deal.

In my lifetime, I have heard an unbelievable amount of nonsense from record company A&R people. One guy, who was supposed to be listening to what I had brought in, started telling me about the various career moves he had made within the record company and concluded by saying that it was a good occupation because there had never been any trouble with his superannuation! Rock'n'roll was indeed here to stay.

I was not prepared, however, for the RODEO reception. One American was at least honest. He acknowledged that Pat's voice was exceptional but said 'the kid sounds black' and, displaying either superhuman ignorance of rock history, or simple racism, rejected him for that reason. Others turned it down out of hand, and one – David Bates at Phonogram – demonstrated traditional ambivalence by announcing that the song was not good enough and that it would have to be re-recorded anyway. The logic of re-recording a bad song still escapes me.

Larry accompanied me on the next trip, and Stiff Records signed it on one hearing. Unfortunately, they then raised everyone's hopes by getting MIDGE URE to produce it, spent a few thousand quid, and didn't release it.

'I never had any music training, but my mother spent years in Naples as a nurse, and was a great opera lover, and would sing around the house. My father was the biggest Frank Sinatra fan out, so he would guide me on to the floor at Christmas parties to sing Frank Sinatra songs . . . at a silly age, two or three, and I would spout *Come Fly With Me* in my baby voice. I hated doing it and rebelled about the age of ten. Then, at 15, when I was making music with my brother Gregory, I realised that all this Frank Sinatra training was really quite good and I started to show off. People then couldn't get me off the floor. It was great for my pitch, timing and phrasing. We went to see him at Ibrox and my father had a great time.

I didn't learn an instrument. My mother's parents had a piano which came to our house. I used to pick out tunes, then Gregory wanted lessons. He mastered the piano, and wanted a saxophone . . . and my mother did a paper round to get it for him. When he was 13 or 14, he began to play sax with a kind of Gothic punk band – VALERIE AND THE WEEK OF WONDERS – whose guitarist, BRIAN MacPHEE now plays with the BIG DISH. I was on the periphery of that, saying, "Do you want a singer?"

I think because I was such an unsociable child – I used to have more communication with the bedroom mirror than with human beings – I would read and fantasise that I was STEVIE WONDER, FRANK SINATRA, MARVIN GAYE, SAM COOKE, and think: "Why do people think I'm so hackit and unsociable when actually I know I'm the greatest talent that ever lived?" That went on for a while and, at first, Greg would always say I was a crap singer. He liked ska *(1979/80)* and I was listening to pop stuff, Frank Sinatra and a BOBBY DARIN record *Winners*. I got into early SIMPLE MINDS because I thought I was supposed to . . . peer group pressure . . . then IAN DURY AND THE BLOCKHEADS and SCRITTI POLITTI. Suddenly, Gregory stopped telling me I was a crap singer and suggested we get together in a band.

He was then in a band called the WINNING LOSERS and they needed a singer. We immediately started to dominate things and got thrown out! It was 1981/82, the first two or three years of my time at university, and we then decided we should do something together. I was beginning to seek out music I'd always liked – STEVIE WONDER'S *Inner Visions*, AVERAGE WHITE BAND'S *Feel No Fret* – but really, I was drawing off limited musical resources.

At school I was always a swot and misfit and, because of that, a homosexual by reputation! I did well academically, though, and took solace in that. I did English Literature, Language and Media Studies at Glasgow University.

Anyway, we called our band UNITY EXPRESS, and did some recording with a pal bass player at Palladium in Edinburgh. We were also tying in with our manager,

Alan MacNeill at this time *(1983)*, who would give us dead time in the middle of the night at his studio in Berkeley Street. It became HUE AND CRY, but I was getting a bit fed up with it and got involved with the group, RODEO, through an ex-school pal who told me they were looking for a singer.

My first impression of the whole experience was "this is not the business for me" and afterwards I decided to chuck it and go back to university. It seemed to make the people around me so craven. MIDGE URE was regarded as this demi-god because he was producing a single. His ideas were not what I would have done and I was also disappointed that I was regarded as a bit player. I felt that if I was going to be in the music business – which I really wanted – it was as a main player. Midge Ure's work was just so far away from my co-ordinates of balladry and Seventies funk, I felt it was just a technical exercise on his part. I sounded like an alien being.

So when I came back, I said to Gregory, "Right, let's make this a bit more serious." We confirmed our relationship with Alan MacNeill, and I got my degree in 1985.

Soon afterwards, we got our publishing deal with Chappell Music. That gave us a couple of thousand, a minimal stipend every week, and money for demos. Then Joan, my wife to be, got a place at journalism college at the City University in London. I went with her and tried to be a media critic for the rock press. Gregory then would come down and we would write in a writing room at Chappell's. Tin Pan Alley. We also got free demo time, so Alan would come with Greg to our flat in Tufnell Park, then meet record companies. Towards the end of Joan's course, we signed with the independent Circa Records *(1986)*.

We got some of the band through adverts in the Mitchell Library – NIGEL CLARK *(guitar)*, JAMES FINNEGAN *(bass)* and DAVID PRESTON *(vocals)*. The choice of a male backing singer was partly musical – our voices worked well together – but also sexuo-political. The last thing I wanted was some kind of ethnic dolly bird backing singer who gave the pallid white guy some credibility. We hoped to get two men, but got one who could take the harmonies up with the requisite quality. We were all listening to early SLY STONE, early STEVIE WONDER, early TEMPTATIONS, and I think that comes out on the first album. And of course, Gregory listens to keyboard players – HERBIE HANCOCK, OSCAR PETERSON.

We did the first album half in Ca Va Studios and half in New York. Producers Jimmy Biondo Lillo and Harvey Goldberg were suggested by the record company and they wanted to get New York horns and strings, and New York mixing desks. The city had been part of my personal imagination for many years and it felt unreal – every move was for some unseen camera – and it was a good environment in which to make music. We could look out of the window of Jimmy's flat and see the Brill Building.

It was only with the second album, though, and with a lot of demoing in between, that we and Gregory in particular, began to come to terms with production. And when we went to LA there was slight culture shock because of thedifferences in the way these people work and the way we work. We did get the money, though, to make the kind of album we wanted, second time around.

Again it was a learning experience. We wanted to get the best American musicians – MICHAEL BRECKER, RON CARTER etc, and it was amazing. As well as giving us a good album, it gave us a standard by which to judge all future musical work. Although we were still not really in control of the process. Our next album may reach platinum status over there although apart from the DANNY WILSON single, no current Scottish band has taken America.'

> PAT KANE at the time of writing enjoys a high profile in Scotland. As well as having been elected Rector of Glasgow University, he writes a column for the *Scotsman* newspaper, and is active in Nationalist politics. We discussed the current situation.

'I'm often asked in London "Why all the 'sincere soul' *(in Scotland)* and no art rock?" and I think it's something to do with the *zeitgeist* of Scottish culture in the mid-Eighties. People are now feeling quite happy about being Scottish whereas previously they might have been regarded as inarticulate, and that went for literature as well as music. Also, money was coming up here and staying in Scotland. My theory of Scottish soul is that it's urban folk music. And soulfulness is speaking truly about yourself and the world, and that's also a Scottish thing, although the house bands that are coming out of Edinburgh now . . . Edinburgh is a far more blandly metropolitan city.

Post-punk in the media was also important. That politicisation of the atmosphere linked in with a parallel development towards cultural autonomy. I would never live in London again. There are both practical – health – and artistic reasons – studios – for staying in Scotland, and it ultimately gives the artiste more control if he can "master" here.

I always had an interest in politics. Of course, because people buy your records, it doesn't mean that they agree with the whole panoply of your artistic sensibilities. Particularly in the south-east of England. In Scotland, however, I have felt that the air that one breathes is anti-Thatcherite and about Scottish self-determination. I feel that I'm expressing viewpoints that most Scots have about

144

their political and economic destinies.'

> I felt obliged to point out that while most Scots may indeed share Pat's viewpoints, they overwhelmingly entrust their political and economic destinies to the Labour Party in Scotland. His view is that things are changing.

'Most young people want some form of self-determination and at least it's nice to have a shared political consensus. As an artiste, though, I'd like to expand a bit . . . if you are a good global artiste, you give your country a certain dignity.

Musically, in Scotland I'm listening to a lot of folk music, and I like people who are undiscovered. I would like MICHAEL MARRA *(see Chapter 22)* to get the right kind of producer. I mean, when I think of the influence he's had on RICKY ROSS and myself . . .'

HUE & CRY
CIRCA RECORDS

Left: LORNA
BROOKS L. BROOKS

Right: HILARY
BROOKS H. BROOKS

CAROL LAULA'S
(MATERNAL)
FAMILY (1918)
C. LAULA

CHAPTER NINETEEN

WOMEN IN SCOTTISH ROCK MUSIC

Introduction

Until the early Eighties, neither Aberdeen nor women had made much impact on Scottish rock music. This, however, was to change with the arrival of ANNIE LENNOX.

Trained[?] as a classical musician, she was converted to popular music – significantly, in Scottish terms – by the musical and production values of STEVIE WONDER. An important personal and professional alliance was then established with Geordie DAVE STEWART and, following the modest success of their TOURISTS group, they became absorbed in contemporary European electronic music and emerged as the EURYTHMICS, an increasingly video-led concept which enjoyed international success.

ANNIE LENNOX is now regarded as one of the world's leading female vocalists and is frequently cited – along with CHRISSIE HYNDE – as someone who has had a great influence on women in the Scottish music scene. She was expecting a baby when I made contact with her office and politely declined an interview.

Working Musicians

HILARY and LORNA BROOKS are sisters from Eaglesham and currently active in the Scottish scene – Lorna as a band vocalist and session singer, and Hilary as a keyboard player and theatrical musical director.

HILARY BROOKS: 'All the women in our family were musical, but none of the men. Both grandmothers played piano to a good standard although they didn't go to college but our mother, who's now a retired music teacher, did, with Alexander Gibson. Our father worked in Glasgow's fruitmarket.

Both of us were encouraged to play from an early age – there were always a lot of instruments in the house – and mainly studied piano.'

LORNA BROOKS: 'I also played trumpet and a bit of violin and recorder. I played in school orchestras and things like the Glasgow Youth Band which was a pool from schools all over Glasgow. I went to Germany with them, playing trumpet. It was an American-style concert band.'

HILARY BROOKS: 'I was more piano, guitar . . . and violin which I played badly in school orchestras and didn't particularly enjoy. Then my brother bought me the sheet music of *Get Back* when I was about seven and I couldn't play it, but that started me and then I was into ELTON JOHN and all these things.'

LORNA BROOKS: 'Both of us had piano lessons but I was more into playing by ear and I started buying records when I was 13 or 14. I was always singing, but I was about 21 before I got into "better" pop music, like JONI MITCHELL.'

HILARY BROOKS: 'I carried on with piano lessons through school because I changed to a good teacher who stopped exams for a while and, around the age of 14, everything became really important. I had a great thirst for music and practised piano for five hours a day, then another hour of violin, and clarinet which I did for two years as well . . . I also did some classical guitar and my hobby, if you like, was JAMES TAYLOR and things like that.

When I was 17 I went to the Glasgow Academy of Music and Drama, then Jordanhill – teacher training – which I don't want to remember. I wanted to play piano in a pub, but I never knew how to go about it. I was offered teaching practice in Strathclyde but I wanted to go somewhere where I would be given free rein in terms of teaching practice and this turned out to be Uist.

It was a bit scary, I was only 20 and some of the kids were 16 and 17 and I ended up in Paible teaching 'O' grade music, which had never been done before. Then I began to develop an interest in doing "shows" with Gaelic material and I also set up a Gaelic choir for Mods because there was a huge wealth of traditional singing on the particular side of the island where I was living.

The Gaelic music was head-opening stuff and it still comes to me in some of the band's *(AH UM)* improvised material, although I think you need to know a lot about it to mix styles. Anyway, I was six and a half years in Uist – mad, pioneering stuff – and I thought it was absolutely gorgeous.'

LORNA BROOKS: 'During this time I left school and went to Dundee College of Education to do a one-year music course. In that time I was in my first-ever band – jazz-funk and I played bass guitar – but didn't play very often and I didn't see much music in Dundee either, although RICKY ROSS was a student at the same college

(1979/80). So I came back to Glasgow and, after a couple of years, I joined a punk band by chance. They were called the PLASTIC FLIES and I played trumpet! We did trendy pubs like the Rock Garden and a new-wave thing was happening but I wasn't a fan of that stuff until I progressed myself. I did like THE PRETENDERS and ANNIE LENNOX, though.

From that three of us formed another band – BACK AT THE FRONT – and I went from trumpet to keyboards and backing vocals. I bought a synth and from there it was into JULIA PLEASE where I was the lead vocalist. I was always the only woman in these bands and a bit green. I was often creative but really just did what I was told. In JULIA PLEASE, however, I was the lead vocalist and main writer. I was getting more confident and knew what I wanted.

We got quite a lot of interest but things were mainly London-orientated. There was some Glasgow management interest but their attitudes were all image and no depth. I mean, I'm willing to compromise artistically but I'm not prepared to put on a wee, short skirt and sing naff songs to make my living in music.

I met CAROL *(LAULA)* during that period *(1985)* and did some backing vocals for her band, THIS PERFECT HEART. We became friends and I also started doing sessions and jingles. TERRY NEASON and I worked on JOHN MARTYN's album *Sapphire* and all this gave me great experience, although I was still working – civil servant in the Department of Energy. I just gave that up a couple of years ago. I have my own band now – BROOKS – and the theatre work I've done with Wildcat has got me my Equity card.'

HILARY BROOKS: 'I came back from Uist in 1986. The teachers' strike had put a ban on extra-curricular teaching so I had had the time to write some songs and Lorna and I did a demo in Skye. Then I went to the Edinburgh Festival – which showed me that I had a lot to learn – but at the end of 1986 I was offered an MD job at the Royal Lyceum. It took some brass neck but I soon discovered that it was just what I had been doing in Uist except on a more professional level. Immediately after that I joined an agency in Edinburgh and a month later I was off to Tahiti with a violinist who had worked on Cunard cruises for 14 years. We did light classical concerts – three a fortnight – whilst we cruised around the world!

When I came back after a year and a half I did the incidental music for *Charlie's Aunt* at the Lyceum, then I was offered an MD job with Borderline and Morag Fullerton. Next I met the guys in AH UM who were looking for a keyboard player – that was a couple of years ago – and I also scored a show, *Butterfly Children*, directed by Dougie Squires . . . brilliant guy! Then it was the Wildcat show *Cleaning Up* for six female voices, and I'm currently in panto and soon to be working live with TERRY NEASON.

In the business I have suffered absolutely no prejudice on account of my sex, particularly in the jazz group. You're either a musician or you're not a musician. And you're either a good one or a bad one. These are the only criteria. We have a residency at Blackfriars in Glasgow.'

LORNA BROOKS: 'Glasgow was the place to be from SIMPLE MINDS onwards . . . until about two years ago. Despite the Year of Culture, the gigs are tailing off. There's a lack of venues.'

CAROL LAULA

'I was born in 1963 in Johnstone. My father's family is of Irish origin and the name is actually Lawler. Some promoter got the wrong spelling from my manager of the time – Alan Gilfillan of Burn One Records – and when I saw "Laula" I just thought it was great.

My mother comes from a gypsy family. Her grandfather – Stefan Georgevich – was a Romany gypsy from Austria and her grandmother came from Poland. When they first came to Scotland they settled in Wick and Stefan's name was taken down as George Veitch. So Veitch became the family name and, around the turn of the century, my grandfather moved down to Paisley, to Backsneddon Street where there was a showground and caravans. He left the caravan when he married, though, and the travelling existence ended there.

Both families were musical. My father's father is a good singer and my mother's sister, when she emigrated to Canada, played piano on an afternoon radio programme. She and my mother would sing duets of Catholic hymns and, in fact, my mother sang all the time, so I don't remember music making any sudden impact on me. I remember being wakened up to hear MARY HOPKIN's single *Those Were The Days* and I liked the OSMONDS and the BAY CITY ROLLERS, then GILBERT O'SULLIVAN. When I was about ten or 11, my Auntie Betty came back from Canada and she sang *Frankie And Johnny* accompanying herself on a guitar. I was stunned. She was a really good singer and player and I wanted to do that.

I had taken guitar lessons at primary school but they didn't last and academically I wasn't very good, although my brothers were clever and the family was quite open-minded. I didn't collect records much either and when people liked the charts, I was listening to JONI MITCHELL. Still am.

I started writing songs around 1979 but they weren't very good so I just began learning other people's songs and I didn't write anything again until 1987. It wasn't because of punk . . . I hated that. I always liked "real" songs – CARLY SIMON, CAROLE KING. Nothing out of the ordinary.

When I left school I went to the Reid Kerr College in Paisley for a year's secretarial course. I hated it, but while I was there I joined my first band, singing. It was called PLAYING FOR TIME. Then I got a job with the House of Fraser and I worked there for four years, keeping the band going. At the end of that period I joined another band called THIS PERFECT HEART.

My mother and father had split up by this time but my father recognised that I was quite serious about music and when I gave up my job and went on the dole, he kept me going. I started writing melodies for this group and we did some reasonable gigs . . . the Mayfair and so forth, but we fell out and, with the next group – TOUCH – I got some studio time from Sean O'Donnell at Chrysalis. This brought me into contact with Duncan and Johnny Cameron at the Evenload studio in East Kilbride and soon *(1989)* I decided to go solo. I did a lot of live work and one song – *Standing Proud* – was chosen as the Glasgow song for 1990. It was produced by Frankie Miller and was supposed to be part of a TV campaign, but the Saatchi agency was in financial trouble and it didn't happen. The whole thing was good for me though and, from working in the Ca Va Studios I got two songs on the Ca Va Sessions album. I'm now doing stuff with Robin Rankin there.

So, next there was a band with JOHNNY CAMERON, HILARY BROOKS, MARTIN HANLON from the SILENCERS and ALAN HOSIE and, on the last tour, NIGEL CLARK was the guitarist and Martin has become the manager.

Women seem to have a bit more space now and I have more confidence generally. I've also done some busking in Paris and I want to get to that big world out there. Having said that, I like a lot of stuff that's going on in Scotland too. I love WET WET WET – I like their attitude – and, if I like folk as people I can always find something in their music. I have also been asked to do a Burns radio programme, which sounds interesting.'

PROCLAIMERS
CHRYSALIS RECORDS

*KENNY
MacDONALD*

CHAPTER TWENTY

KENNY MACDONALD

'On a night of a full moon in Waterford . . .'

KENNY MacDONALD manages the PROCLAIMERS. He has seen them rise from support group in an Edinburgh pub to one of Scotland's top-selling international groups.

'I was born in Ellon in 1956 but at the age of four we moved to Singapore where my father was a civil servant working with the forces. Out there you could have a luxurious life-style on an average wage. I remember seeing *A Hard Day's Night* once, when there was fighting going on in the street and they had to abandon it halfway through. My father came originally from Stornoway and the music he liked was Calum Kennedy, Kenneth MacKellar and Andy Stewart. My older sister had BEATLES and ELVIS records, though, and I remember being quite excited by the *Shindig* TV programme that came from the States.

We came back to East Kilbride when I was 11 and the weather and quality of life were something of a culture shock. I was viewed as a curiosity and lived off the "mysteries of the Orient" for some time. And I hadn't been exposed to football much, so I embraced that with great passion.

Musically, it was chart stuff. I would buy one album every six months and I suppose I knew what I didn't like: YES, PINK FLOYD and EMERSON LAKE & PALMER. The first stuff I really liked was the glitter period – BOWIE and MOTT THE HOOPLE – and the SENSATIONAL ALEX HARVEY BAND was the first band I worshipped. You could go to a friend's house four afternoons a week and sit listening to the same album – *Next,* or DAVID BOWIE.

After my 'O' grades I left school and worked as a civil servant for a year with Hamilton District but I realised I wasn't cut out for that and I started selling central heating and then encyclopaedias. This let me travel around Scotland and we hit a goldmine in the fishing communities in the north-east – Peterhead to Tain. You only got paid for what you sold, so this brought out the entrepreneur in me.

From there I went to Aberdeen but property was expensive so I went up to the oil terminal at Flotta in Orkney. They had an entertainments complex and this would have been the first real work I did in the entertainments area but I got involved in the unionisation of the catering people and received a police escort off the island!

Next I went to work in a holiday camp in Great Yarmouth and once, when I was in Wales, I remember hearing the JAM on a jukebox in Wrexham. Punk music was becoming a kind of backdrop and, when I came back to Glasgow *(1976)*, I really embraced this music. I was working as a trainee manager with Oddbins and, for going to the pub, I made up a jacket of binbags and safety pins. The first punk in Byres Road!

Then I started going to gigs in Glasgow and Edinburgh and buying singles again and, when I located myself in Edinburgh I became involved with a flatmate who was in a band – the DEAF JERKS from Falkirk. I saw how badly organised they were and began to help them with this. I suppose it was my first taste of rock'n'roll. The bass player then went to a better band – NEON BARBS – and I started to get more seriously interested in music as a profession. I was losing substantial sums of my own money but I managed to establish my own label and we got a *Melody Maker* "single of the week". You were suddenly starting to see bands emerge locally – the REVILLOS and the SKIDS – everyone previously had left Scotland.

In 1983, however, faced with a mortgage and family to keep, I ended up opening a restaurant – Lilligs in Victoria Street – which I ran for four years and part of the speciality was the music played. A lot of musicians hung out there and this kept me in touch with what was going on. I got involved with another band – LONGER AT THE FRONT – and dabbled in gigs and clubs. Then through the restaurant connection I heard a demo which a friend, Terry Adams, had made of these two guys – twins – from Fife, but who now lived in Edinburgh. This was the PROCLAIMERS and I thought it was wonderful. The tape had most of the songs that went on the first album – *Letter From America* was there, only rougher and louder.

They had left Auchtermuchty when they left school. They were in bands – the HIPPIE HASSLERS, BLACK FLAG and REASONS FOR EMOTION – but found that internal democracy hadn't worked for them. Also they hadn't done much singing in these bands. CRAIG *(REID)* was a drummer and CHARLIE a guitarist and when they started doing their own songs they felt a bit stupid slipping into American accents. So they stuck with their natural, Scots, voices. It wasn't a political thing although they had been young SNP activists. I mean, their folks had been traditional Labour voters and JAMES BROWN was a favourite in their record collection. It was just the way things worked out.

So I just played this tape all the time. I made copies for my friends and we would have PROCLAIMERS parties after hours in the restaurant. It was the power and

quality of the songs ... there was novelty in the subject matter but it was the
passion and the performance I liked.

A year later, I was walking down Victoria Street and I saw this blackboard
outside Nicky Tam's pub – the CATERAN supported by the PROCLAIMERS. They had
previously had no profile so I was excited and got hold of a couple of mates. Now,
at last, here were these two faces ... in front of seven Goths! They were dressed
similarly but not identically, but it was like a Hollywood thing ... I thought they
were superstars and resolved to do whatever it would take.

I went up to them afterwards and virtually embraced them and, the next day I
offered to put up £1,000 for a single. But they weren't interested. They wanted a
major deal. So I just went to see them as a fan from then onwards and they were
slowly picking up interest. By the end of 1986, I had learned more about managing
bands – I treated *Music Week* and books and so forth like a kind of course – and they
obviously began to see potential managerial qualities in me. I think their previous
manager, Kai Davidson, was more of a friend, and I tried to get Bruce Findlay
(SIMPLE MINDS) or Bob Last *(HUMAN LEAGUE)* to manage them, but they didn't
respond.

PROCLAIMERS
CHRYSALIS RECORDS

155

Luckily, they got a break supporting the HOUSEMARTINS on 15 dates and I took a holiday to drive them. On a night of a full moon in Waterford *(Ireland)* they asked me to manage them.

So, in the winter of 1986, I decided to give up my active role in the restaurant and everybody told me I was mad . . . but I couldn't see anything other than the PROCLAIMERS. Eventually, after weeks of hammering away, I got them on the TUBE and, the next day, the phone went 18 times instead of the normal once.

A guy called John Williams signed them to Chrysalis and produced the first album. There was no great marketing ploy – it was just the guys' natural image and the "live" thing was building up. People said that England and the English press would hate us, but the opposite was the case . . . we were really hip!

The second album sold a million and it was like Beatlemania in Australia and Canada. And it's not Scottish-based. Most gigs would have a few drunk Jocks but the US media, for example, thinks they're Irish and it's just regular Americans at the gigs.

In terms of record sales, we sell more internationally than any Scottish band except SIMPLE MINDS. But they're not Scots zealots. It's just a continuation of their lives and who they are . . . and their musical development will come naturally.

Also, they could be on chat shows all the time, but they're not BILLY BRAGG or PAT KANE. Their political activities are those of private individuals and the political side of their music is really only a small part. Some journalists think it's 95 per cent.'

CHAPTER TWENTY-ONE

WET WET WET

MARTI PELLOW AND GRAEME CLARK

'When you see somebody smilin', you smile yourself'

WET WET WET were a major teen phenomenon of the 1980s and probably the most successful Scottish group in the UK market at that time, selling almost two million copies of their début album. They are more interesting for two other reasons, however: their musical ability, which belies their teen image and tender years, and their decision, along with manager, Elliot Davis, to set up their own business infrastructure in Scotland from the word go. They now operate from an office, rehearsal and state-of-the-art recording complex in the West End of Glasgow.

'We were all born around 1964/65. We're all the same age, all went to the same school and all our parents worked in shipbuilding and construction trades . . . in Clydebank.'

MARTI PELLOW: 'Music was really just my parents' record collection and my mother did a little bit of singing. Big band sound, that sort of thing. So she was my main influence and, when people came over, it was the TV turned off, a wee drink and singing. So I was always surrounded by that type of entertainment . . . and Pellow was my mother's maiden name. It's Yugoslavian, my real name is MacLachlan . . . Pellow was just something that I used.'

GRAEME CLARK: 'My grandfather played the piano in cinemas before there was sound. My mother's father . . . and he had come to Glasgow from Leadhills in the Borders to work in the shipyards. Neil's *(NEIL MITCHELL, keyboards)* is from Lossiemouth and Tom's *(TOM CUNNINGHAM, drummer)* from Govan . . . people came to Clydebank from all over.'

MARTI PELLOW: 'People would also travel from quite far away on a daily basis. It was a boom town with the yards and Singer's sewing machines. Then, during the war the town was bombed . . .'

GRAEME CLARK: ' . . . so our first band was called the CLYDEBANK BLITZ. It was the punk thing.

My father died when I was eight but my mother played the piano a bit. I think she thought that her father could have done better as a musician if he had got the chance, so she had an interest in it as far as I was concerned. After we left school we all went on the dole and it was hard for our mothers but our parents all liked music and dancin' and they believed in us.'

MARTI PELLOW: 'On a Friday night we wouldna' be goin' out for a few drinks . . . we would sit in and try to get songs together.'

GRAEME CLARK: 'We met at Clydebank High an' I met Tommy when he moved from Drumchapel to Hardgate.'

MARTI PELLOW: 'Bought hooses . . .'

GRAEME CLARK: 'Aye, middle class. Tommy played drums, his father had bought him a kit for £20, and I played bass.'

MARTI PELLOW: 'I was just singin' . . . and I was always a character who sought attention, even at school. Graeme an' me were in the same fitba' team – Goldenhill – a Boys Club-type team. I would sing songs in the dressin' rooms . . . I didn't know if it was like the record or not . . . you just take it for granted, so I'm singin' DIONNE WARWICK or MICHAEL JACKSON or somethin' and Graeme says, "Oh aye? That's aw right." When I was young we had 78s . . . PATSY CLINE, VICKI CARR . . . ballads. My mum could really sing the standards.'

GRAEME CLARK: 'So Tommy was playin' the *(social)* clubs and I got him up to my house. We were, like, 14 . . . my bass had three strings cos you've no' got a tenner when you're 14 . . . But the punk thing said anyone could do it, so we had to get songs. That was the way ahead. I liked the CLASH . . . I saw them at the Apollo in 1978. And I liked the BEATLES when I was younger. And, of course, DAVID BYRNE of TALKING HEADS, who came originally from Dumbarton. They were the real punks.'

MARTI PELLOW: 'I was always interested in singers, be it TOM JONES or JAMES BROWN. The punk attitude was appealing to me but I had grown up listening to melody and the punk songs were a wee bit blue murder. We used to share records and when we looked at our record collections it was black music.'

GRAEME CLARK: 'The CLYDEBANK BLITZ must have been about 1979. We tried to write our own songs and we did CLASH songs . . . there was a guitarist as well at that time . . . but we were also listening to MICHAEL JACKSON and BURT BACHARACH, so the ideas were maybe half-baked but we were forced to mature. We played at school discos but, when we left school, the Tories had come in and the economic climate was bad *(1980/81)*. All we wanted to do was play music. We were offered YOP schemes and we did jobs for demo money . . . we went to Centre City Sound in Glasgow . . . then we got the £7 sleeper bus to London. Leave at 10 p.m. and arrive at six in the morning feeling like shit. We hawked the tapes around . . . we hadn't even told our parents we had gone and someone took photographs and we were found out! Anyway, we actually went to Phonogram and played the tape to Ashley Goodall who told us to use a better tape machine. The guy at Rough Trade – Geoff Travis – also took an interest, which gave us some hope.'

159

MARTI PELLOW: 'We still didn't have a name, though, and WET WET WET maybe came from a SCRITTI POLITTI song " . . . face wet, wet with tears". Double names were popular – DURAN DURAN, THE THE, TALK TALK – so we went one better! But there was nothing in the name . . . it was the music.'

GRAEME CLARK: 'The soul thing came through in Marti's voice but I think we also had a British song-writing feel – SQUEEZE, ELVIS COSTELLO, KINKS – classic British writing. Keep that identity but have a singer who sounded black.'

MARTI PELLOW: 'At the first-ever "real" gig . . . we had been workin' for umpteen years gettin' the songs to the best of our ability . . . we played at the Multi-media club in Sauchiehall Street. 1984, maybe. It was a Wednesday night and Elliot *(Davis, manager)* managed the resident band, SUNSET GUN . They did the whole night with breaks, maybe for a comedian, then us. The gear was set up and all we had to take were drumsticks and guitars. We had never played on a stage before and we thought we were "there". I fell, or something, at one point and I remember Elliot standing over me saying, "That was a good gig".'

MARTI PELLOW: 'The sheer youth and enthusiasm . . . we were naïve. When Elliot's deal fell through, he phoned us up. He was thinking about management consultancy at the time.'

GRAEME CLARK: 'We went to meet him and there were another two bands – MOROCCAN COCOA and the FLOOR. Elliot played us off against each other to get us working.'

MARTI PELLOW: 'Whoever got the deal was gonna be the band to sort out everyone else on the Precious label. Use the money. We did loads of showcase gigs and, really, we were the ace in the pack because we were younger and ultimately had teenage appeal. And songs like *Angel Eyes* and *Sweet Little Mystery* had taken shape, even at that time.

A year later, we demoed it with Wilf Smarties at his Planet studio in Edinburgh. That was the first time we were in a real studio with a real producer.'

The first album . . .

GRAEME CLARK: 'We were railroaded by the record company to go in and work with

160

a producer who was, basically, a fat American bastard. David Bates *(Phonogram)* set the guy up – he had just had a number one in Europe with ANIMATION's *Obsession* – so we met him, went to the Manor studio, and what you don't realise is that, this wonderful studio . . . this guy drivin' around in a big hire car . . . *you're* payin' for it!

A week into it we were gettin' bad vibes. We went to the record company and said, "This is not happening". It was an expensive mistake but you've got to learn. We asked to do it ourselves, Bates said OK, but when we came back to him *(with a Wilf Smarties' production)* he played about two and a half minutes of it then ejected it and threw it at us. That was the turning point. We had lost respect for him.'

The first album . . . Part II . . .

MARTI PELLOW: 'So then, Willie Mitchell's name came up again. When we first got our deal wi' Phonogram, we drew up a short list of producers and the reaction was, "What? These guys haven't had a hit in 20 years!" Willie Mitchell *(AL GREEN's producer)* was one of them. So a year down the line, when our publisher – Jill Steen – heard of the hassles we were havin', she got a tape to him.'

GRAEME CLARK: 'He said, "Yeh, the singer can sing, why don't you get them over and we'll have a chat?" We thought . . . "too right!"'

MARTI PELLOW: 'Graeme and I went to meet him in Memphis . . . I mean, there would have been no point in goin' in, settin' up the gear and hopin' for the best! When he talked to us, he was nervous too. He's an older man but, as soon as we started talkin' about music, he started to get a "feel" for us and said, "How come you know all our music, man? You guys weren't even born!" I mean, the man was a legend in our record collection!

The studio is an old cinema hall in South Lauderdale which, in the Twenties and Thirties, was white territory which they subsequently abandoned and now it's a black ghetto. Willie is involved in the community, though, and not only did we not have any hassle, we went to his house and ate with him . . . Papa Willie . . . catfish, gumbo . . .

In the studio it was everybody in one room, gettin' the feel . . . a song every couple of days, with just a few overdubs. It was only 16-track, though, and he did have a bit of techno-fear.'

GRAEME CLARK: 'New bands were workin' in state-of-the-art studios but we wanted to get back to the sound of the great songs and try to make *our* songs timeless.'

MARTI PELLOW: 'It's still the same place . . . same mikes, same horns *(Memphis Horns)* that AL GREEN etc used . . . some of them had played in Scotland with the Soul Revues.

We were happy with the exercise as a learning process. We had had the flash producer, we had met the legend . . . now we wanted to reach a happy medium and bring things together.'

The first album . . . Part III

MARTI PELLOW: 'Michael Baker came out of Boston . . . great feel . . . and Axel Kroll was a great programmer. They were a good combination and we worked well with them although the songs have never changed dramatically . . .'

GRAEME CLARK: '*Home And Away (Angel Eyes)* was the very first song that we thought would do well. It worked, even in the bedrooms.

The first single was *Wishin' I Was Lucky* – the same recording by Wilf Smarties that David Bates had thrown back in our faces. We took the tape, did some overdubs and re-mixed it. I suppose it was rope to hang us with . . . Then we did *Sweet Little Mystery* with the two guys and, eventually, the rest of the album including some stuff by ourselves at Castle Sound. And, as we were growing as musicians, so Elliot was developing as a businessman. And we would think up promotion schemes together. We had four hits from the album *Popped In Souled Out,* sold just under two million copies and it was Phonogram's largest-selling début album, ever. The brain damage was worth it.'

MARTI PELLOW: 'We released *The Memphis Sessions* after the album, but with no singles . . . we didnae want people to perceive it as "the new album".'

On the business decision to consolidate their operation in Scotland . . .

MARTI PELLOW: 'We always wanted to stay based in Scotland . . . have our own people around us and not just be a name on a roster. SIMPLE MINDS and BIG COUNTRY had proved that you could have success and stay at home. We also liked the Postcard idea and wanted to take it a stage farther. And then, of course, we wanted to do something for the fans in Scotland, so we did the Glasgow Green concert . . .

We hope the young fans will move with us.'

GRAEME CLARK: 'The reaction of the fans was always good . . . colleges and places . . . although we had our own people from Clydebank and Glasgow at these gigs. Things really started happening for us after we did our first *Top of the Pops* and the Scottish media – BBC Scotland, Radio Clyde – were also supportive at that time. After *Wishin' I Was Lucky,* things were really good . . . the Pavilion, in Glasgow . . . Marti would be nervous an' smile and, when you see somebody smilin' you smile yourself.

We produced *Hold Back The River*, the second album ourselves, and we're currently about 50 per cent into the third one. We're big in Europe, but still not placed in the States although we've toured with ELTON JOHN . . . Hollywood Bowl, four nights at Madison Square Garden . . . and, hopefully, we'll go over again and work at it . . .'

ELLIOT DAVIS – *MD 'PRECIOUS'*

'I was on my third warning at the dole . . .'

'I was born in 1958 and my family was certainly not musical. My parents were divorced when I was seven and my mother brought up myself and my two brothers. She worked as a saleswoman in Mona Lewis and Crazy House. I'm Jewish and, four generations ago, my ancestors came from Russia and Poland. Somewhere down the line there's a Rabbi in the family, but I have no particular religious leanings.

I grew up in Glennap Street, off Albert Drive, and went to Pollokshields Primary. When my mother remarried, we moved to Shawlands and I went to Shawlands Academy. My older brother worked in a record shop and one day they gave me a Saturday job. I remember rolling posters and putting them into polythene bags. My brother was a music fanatic and one of my parents' friends ran a jeweller's which was owned by the people who owned Greens Playhouse, so we would get to the concerts. I remember going to see SLADE, GARY GLITTER, SPARKS, COCKNEY REBEL and so forth, around 1972/73.

163

I was quite brainy at school and I went to Glasgow College of Technology to do opthalmic optics. By that time, though, I was becoming more interested in music. At one point I actually did a gig with a group but I'll say no more on that! I was friendly with a guy whose group had a deal with Factory Records – the WAKE – and I was selling live bootleg cassettes at the universities and wanted to promote concerts. Rob Gretton of NEW ORDER let me promote a few gigs with the WAKE in support and they then asked me to manage them *(1982/83)*. I went on to manage a group called SUNSET GUN and ran a little club – the Wednesday Club – at Night Moves in Sauchiehall Street. The group then got a deal and proceeded to sack me but it was the best thing that could have happened, because I got a financial settlement and set up the Precious Organisation.

After a while I had stopped running the club but it had been the intention to look for more new talent in Glasgow and three or four acts subsequently got record deals, the most successful of whom were WET WET WET. My flatmate, Robert King from Clydebank, had had a really awful tape of this band who I thought had a mediocre singer and pretty average songs! However, I decided to put them on and they came along and were fine . . . 17 years old. We actually videoed it but the guitarist at the time left the tape on a bus. They didn't make much of an impression on me but when the SUNSET GUN thing folded I decided to make contact with both them and a group called SUGAR SUGAR. WET WET WET were actually doing quite well for themselves – Geoff Travis at Rough Trade was showing interest – but he was working with SCRITTI POLITTI and trying to get them away first. By the time he achieved that, I had whipped the group away, although he did actually come up to Glasgow to see them.

SUGAR SUGAR decided to go with Mark Goldinger and CBS so I went for the little band with the crazy, white acoustic piano! I phoned GRAEME CLARK and told him that I had some money and wanted to start a record label with the Wets and a couple of other groups *(1984)*. We were staying at 614 Pollokshaws Road in a room and kitchen and there were always music people either sharing the flat or dropping by . . . Robert *(who went on to form a label called Nexus)*, John Dingwall *(journalist)* and BRIAN SUPERSTAR from the PASTELS.

We were so naïve, we thought we couldn't possibly fail! I thought *my* ideas were so good, I couldn't fail, even although the groups were still mediocre as song-writers.

Within Scotland, the scene was still dead *(1984)*. The Postcard thing was very introverted and amateurish and didn't succeed in getting the big labels interested. I would have these arguments with Alan Horne . . . I mean, John Dingwall was

164

writing for *Sounds,* Tom Morton for *Melody Maker* and Andrea Miller for the *NME.* Three journalists working for the national papers. Why couldn't we get chart hits? We just needed to create the scam and we couldn't fail.

The ongoing premise was that by the time the new label got the publicity, the bands – WET WET WET, MOROCCAN COCO and the FLOOR – would be good enough. We got full-page articles on Precious before we got any deals and meanwhile were spending hours, days, weeks in the bedroom with a porta-studio. They were hard-working and it's not just ability that succeeds. It seemed obvious, though, that if you knew the *right* records and understood the process of making records, you were gonna make good records. It was just a matter of time.

WET WET WET had good melodies and keyboard lines, and Marti's enthusiasm and shyness impressed me. He didn't look or sing like a star. He wouldn't move and never smiled. He did have a voice, though, and somehow had the aura of a star, although the image thing was not part of our thinking at this time. We simply wanted good singers and good songs on Precious. In Wet Wet Wet's case, the songs would start with Neil, and Graeme would be the motivator.

Because of the interest generated in SUNSET GUN, I was quite hot at generating

Early WET WET WET PHONOGRAM RECORDS

165

publicity. A&R men would come to Glasgow on the strength of that, although we were still on the dole. By early 1985, we had been knocked back by a number of record labels . . . and Marti had had an offer to drop me and the band and go solo. Publishing, however, was moving. We did a demo at Wilf Smarties' studio and a girl – Jill Steen from Chrysalis – was showing interest in a song called *Home And Away*. We did a gig in Glasgow and she told me she wanted to sign them for publishing. London Records had also wanted to sign them and John Kennedy *(London music business lawyer)* said, "Maybe we should go for this . . ." I said, "Calm down . . . this is gonna go mega."

By the time we signed with Phonogram, we had seven deals on the table, each of them over £100,000. Publishing also paid £50,000 in the first year which wasn't a massive deal, but Jill was such a doll and she still works with us. We believed in people more than money.

My own "conversion", if you like, came at a gig at Night Moves. The FLOOR were doing psychedelic stuff, years ahead of their time, the place was reasonably busy and the WETS did *I Can Give You Everything*. When the key change came in, Marti hit a fantastic note and myself, Andrea and Tom Morton were of the same opinion . . . we couldn't fail. However, we began to get hordes of A&R men every time we played and the pressure was enormous, not only on ourselves but on the other bands as well, who had interest in their own right. So we agreed to concentrate on the Wets to try and get some money and then help the others.

We stopped doing gigs . . . we did some showcase stuff at Park Lane Studios which were unsuccessful because the "live" magic was missing – although they made us money – and Chrysalis actually decided to pull out of the publishing deal, against Jill's wishes. Warners then offered to double the money and Chrysalis came back *because* Warners were interested. So we signed with them, which gave us breathing space. I was on my third warning at the dole . . .

Eventually, we did a sub-licensing *(record)* deal with Phonogram. There had been an offer from CBS which Marti wanted to go for, but the others didn't and we worked democratically. We wanted to build in Scotland with me acting not as manager, but running the record label and advising them. Setting up a *bona fide* record company and letting London know that if they were not interested in making records, we were, and to hell with them. It worked later with GOODBYE MR MacKENZIE.

With the WETS, the deal with Phonogram was one of the biggest, most comprehensive put together at that time; we did a five-album deal which gave us control over releases of records, marketing, publicity etc, and we brought in

Andrea Miller to handle the PR. I think we were the first company in Scotland to do this and she did a wonderful job. I had known her from Glasgow College days, and she's now a director at the Beeb.'

The first album . . .

David Bates at Phonogram had liked the initial demos but things started to go wrong with his first choice of producer. First there was the incident when he threw the Wilf Smarties tape on the floor, then the Memphis tape was unacceptable and at that point he tried to get rid of me and get us kicked off the label. The Phonogram investment was so huge, however, that David Simone *(Phonogram's MD)* decided to take Bates off the case and give us one last chance to do things ourselves. We spent 25 hours on the re-mix of *Wishing* and I took the tape to Glasgow and played it to Andrea who was always my sounding board. I put it on . . . her face lit up . . . and I knew we had a hit record. Even after it got to number six in the charts, however, there were individuals still trying to stop our choice of follow-up in Europe – *Sweet Little Mystery* – and I believe that at the end of the day, we needed a million album sales to break even. Fortunately, we achieved that and more but it was a while before we saw money from recordings. There was, of course, merchandising and publishing.

After the record deal we set up rehearsal and office space and now we have two 24-track studios. But we're only just starting. We currently employ eight people although the management job is occasionally thankless and I often think of walking away from it, but that's another story.'

Wets in the Park . . .

We wanted to do something unique, spectacular and in Glasgow – which wasn't simply a career move. The free concert *(1989)* attracted 75-100,000 people and cost maybe £170,000 to put on. It was the biggest pop concert ever staged in Scotland and we did a video, but it didn't make money.

America is the next target and it will be Adult Contemporary and Chart Hit Radio which will break the band. Precious will also have another album this year . . . from BOOM . . . and let's not forget WALK DON'T WALK and THE HEADLINE, our latest protégés.

MICHAEL MARRA

M. MARRA

CHAPTER TWENTY-TWO

MICHAEL MARRA

'Song-writing is more important than money'

MICHAEL MARRA comes from the Dundee soul music tradition but has now established himself as a highly original and distinctive songwriter. Perhaps his most remarkable cover version is LEO SAYER singing a tribute to the former Dundee United goalie, Hamish MacAlpine.

The families of both Michael Marra's grandparents came to Dundee from Ireland and his grandfather, Nicholas Marra, was a prominent figure in the disputes which hit the jute industry in the 1920s.

'My father was a letterpress printer, and passionate about music – Duke Ellington and Beethoven – although he never sang until he was about 60. My mother was a good singer, though, in choirs and things and when my father bought a piano, my brother Eddie took it up. He played in a Dundee group in the Sixties called the MILLIONAIRES, and I would play when he was out. He showed me how to play *Go Now* in E-flat and I've been there or thereabouts ever since! I mean, I've written in all keys but E-flat suits my voice now. Another brother, Christopher, plays guitar and recently worked with DANNY WILSON.

I got taught music at school but it was rubbish and I preferred the stuff you would hear in church – the Catholic hymns which, to me, are just hits. Academically, I was first boy in the primary school, but puberty was a great big blur of anarchy and I was in a lot of trouble. I didnae like the nuns as teachers, I came out of the church, and was expelled from school at fourteen. There was nothing for me there, and all they ever told you was . . . "If you have no 'O' levels . . ." I still come away wi' traces o' that yet, for *I have no 'O' Levels (laughs)*. The theatre, of course, is the correct business for people who have no 'O' levels. If you come up with the result, it doesn't matter if you have 'O' levels or not.

From school, my dad got me a job as a message laddie wi' Dundee Printers, and that was great. I had a year there because I couldna' start an apprenticeship until I was 16. I learned every street in Dundee. I was given my bus money to go to Douglas *(outskirts)* and I used to sprint! Keep the money and buy fags. But I learned the town and also met interesting people.

The first band, at school, was the SAINTS. I was about 13 and at one of the annexes of Lawside *(Academy)*, St Joseph's in Blackness Road. We played the Gaumont Saturday Morning club – I played guitar. Then I didn't get to start my apprenticeship wi' the printers because of my school record so, instead, I went to Burnett's the bakers in Clepington Road. This meant my mother had to get up at four in the mornin' to wake me up. I stayed there for a wee while, then I got an apprenticeship as an electrician wi' Kilpatrick in Albert Square. They had a deal wi' the university, so I went to work there for about a year, and that was interesting. Then I left and went to London – with music in mind – when I was 17 *(1969)*.

I was in a flat on Clapham Common wi' five lassies fae farms around Blairgowrie, and they smothered me! I wasn't in a band but there was a gig at the Nag's Head in Wandsworth Road and, one night when I was drunk, I sang *That Lucky Old Sun.* It went down a ton, so I came out feelin' good, for I felt like a hick in London. I stayed in London for 18 months. It was easy to get jobs and there were people from all over the world, which I found very exciting. Musically, JOHN LENNON had introduced me to black music and in Dundee my influences had been the RENEGADES with CLARK and PHIL ROBERTSON *(later SLEAZ BAND)*, the RITE TYME – NORRIE TENNANT, STEWART CUTHBERT, FRANK VETTRAINO and RICKY MUNRO and, of course, the VIKINGS. I went briefly to Holland at this stage, with a friend called Alfie Bremer – his aunt, Lucille Bremer, played Judy Garland's sister in *Meet Me in St Louis* – we were buskin' and livin' in a park.

I wrote songs from the BEATLES on. Seven years old. When I was at primary school and folk said, "What are you gonna be?" I said, "A song-writer." One day this guy says, "My uncle's a song-writer." We say, "What's his name, then?" He says, "Stephen Sondheim." We say, "That'll be right! Never even heard o' 'im!" But it came out of thin air, and turned out to be true. I kept notebooks but later destroyed them, although there was a song I wrote when I was 16 called *Goodnight To Lovely You* that was shortlisted for the *Midas Touch* album. Nowadays things are very different but I'm always in the throes of writing a song. My thing is all about shapes which are never thought of as mathematics. Chord changes suggest melodies, and that for me is the exciting point . . . when you find original melodies, things the tune squad can't pick you up for. Sometimes the melodies can be remarkably simple compared to the changes that found them out.

When I came back to Dundee, the first main band I had was HEN'S TEETH, with my brother, Christopher, and ARLENE GOWANS who subsequently sang on the *Gaels Blue* album. I turned into a bass player because they didnae have one. It was folky and eventually merged with an art college rock'n'roll group called MORT WRIGGLE

AND THE PANTHERS to form SKEETS BOLIVER *(1972/73)* . . . Stuart Ivans, Angus Foye, Chris and myself and Brian MacDermott who is currently with DEL AMITRI. That group got out and about. Stuart Ivans was a good organiser who, like a lot of people, had come to art college and loved Dundee. We made demos and got a place in a talent competition which gave us a record deal with Thunderbird Records in London. It was run by Dick Rowe *(the man who turned down the BEATLES)* and Mick Green, the PIRATES' guitarist. We did a couple of singles and it was exciting working in London. But I didn't want to work on other people's material any more.

I had known RAB NOAKES for a number of years and, in fact, Peg and I spent our honeymoon at his house in Strathmiglo. I had kept contact with him and he was always supportive. BARBARA DICKSON had moved from folk clubs to bands and Rab was involved there, so I sent some stuff to her manager via Rab. Bernard Theobald was his name and I signed to him for publishing, plus he got a record deal with Polydor *(1979)*. At that point I was spending most of my time in London, because it was like a big magnet. Great studios and musicians. I did a vocal session wi' ANNIE ROSS. Great. JIM MULLEN. That was for a second album with MIKE VERNON *(Blue Horizon)*, which never saw the light of day.

Also, I was doing covers . . . FRANKIE MILLER, KIKI DEE, LEO SAYER . . . but they weren't comin' out. BARBARA DICKSON did one, though *(Peter)*, and it went on to a K-TEL album so eventually I paid off my publishing debt, around 1985 or 1986. But it was a nightmare, 'cos I'm hopeless in business and Theobald was involved in management, so he wasn't hustling as he should have done. I also put GARY CLARKE in his direction and that led to a court case.

By then, however, Scottish studios were beginning to open up and, given those circumstances, I thought that records coming out of Scotland would begin to reflect Scotland. It wouldn't be folk in London sayin', "Give us the same song again!" Because that's what they're all about. The musicians and arrangers in London were great but record company people would make you want to be a plumber. I've been pulled up for writing a song which they considered "Scottish". It was called *Like A Frenchman* and was later covered by DAVE KELLY, but they associated GERAINT WATKINS' accordion with Scotland! I began to think I was never gonna get on with these guys, and every company is the same, for they couldnae exist in any other business. So I decided to write Scottish songs and that annoyed my publisher as well. He was like, "What am I supposed to dae wi' this?" *(laughs)*. *General Grant* was the first and, curiously, that was the song that attracted the attention of the theatre people in Dundee.

Gaels Blue was written as a Scottish work but without changing the way I work musically. The subjects were Scottish, historical and so forth. The guys in London forced me into it and it was made for no money, in the knowledge that it would make no money. I could feel all right about it, though – although, subsequently, you doubt that as well – and a definite decision was made that no record company or publisher was gonna have any effect on it. If I never met a publisher again, it wouldna bother me. They normally like one little part of your work which is "commercial", and they want you to continually come up with it.

Anyway, Alan Lyddiard at Dundee Rep was attracted to it – he had moved up from London and asked me to do the music for the Billy Kay play, *They Fairly Mak Ye Work*. It was a big success and afterwards I did two Craigmillar Festival shows. In songwriting terms, you had to write about unusual subjects like damp – I loved it and it was a good education. You had to write, rehearse and perform in three weeks and it was like that SAMMY CAHN quote, that most of his songs started with a phone call. I mean, sometimes lines have taken me months, when pressure would have made it happen quicker.

A Wee Home From Home – the idea was Frank McConnell's. I wrote the music and Gerry Mulgrew, whom I was always hearing about, directed. We went into a room in Paisley every day for six weeks, with a date to open. I found it pretty mental, but journalists would arrive at rehearsals and write glowing reports. I thought, "We'd better start glowin', boys!" It won some money for the company in London, though, and one of the songs was picked up by HUE AND CRY.

RICKY ROSS wrote to me once, when he was younger, asking for some advice. He came up really well, and later he was organising a gig for Nicaragua at the Third Eye. I performed, and PAT KANE stood up and did a couple of songs, unaccompanied. First time I'd heard him and I was knocked out. Then MARTI PELLOW and NEIL MITCHELL did something and that was great, too. From that point on there were various connections. Maybe PAT KANE would gie me some o' his 'O' levels!

After *Your Cheatin' Heart* (BBC-TV), I'd like to go back to the theatre, keep a good distance until it settles. I doubt if I'll ever work on another show like that. So intense, although it was great – John Byrne – and there was money. Also I've got a wee part in the film, *The Big Man*.'

Michael Marra concludes with an anecdote:

'Through Bernard Theobald, I got an offer to write lyrics for Bjorn Ulvaeus of ABBA. I had been working at the Edinburgh Festival and felt so unwell I was seriously worried. I thought the ABBA thing might be worth a few bob for my family, though, so I left Edinburgh and went to work at my mother's hideout at Dunkeld. I worked on this lyric and phoned Bjorn from the box outside Niel Gow's house, played it down the phone and sang. But I would occasionally change the melody and he'd say, "That's not correct." He had it on a computer screen, like I've got now. I was getting no humour from him, his English was poor and I was thinkin' I was gonna die, but I felt I had to make a good job of it. So I carried on and finished it, then came home and went to a doctor. He told me I had an ulcer and it was such a relief. I said I would never, ever do that again. Prostitution. I had kept sayin' . . . "What are we writing about, here? . . . What are you tryin' to say?" He didna' care. All that was important was the syllables, the mathematics, and the intention of making money. I earned nothing and the big lesson was: songwriting is more important than money.'

RUNRIG
CHRYSALIS RECORDS

CHAPTER TWENTY-THREE

RUNRIG

'The Road to Damascus'

Although now based in and around Edinburgh, RUNRIG will forever be identified with the Hebrides, and the Island of Skye. That they should have achieved a UK Top Ten album, become Scotland's top live attraction and re-drawn the map of contemporary Gaelic music must make them arguably the greatest phenomenon in the history of Scottish rock music.

The first time I saw them was in the summer of 1974. I had lived in Skye for two years and toured extensively in the Highlands and Islands with my own band. I knew the members of the group vaguely and somehow we had arranged a support spot for them, for a fee of £15, if my memory serves me correctly.

My own musical background owed virtually everything to black music and my first impression was that although they had a comfortable rhythmic feel, their accordionist was too clumsy and the sound of their vocalist too rounded for them to make any impact in rock music. I could not have been more wrong, for I now believe BLAIR DOUGLAS to be one of the truly outstanding accordionists and, besides coming to appreciate DONNIE MUNRO's treatment of the Gaelic ballads in particular, I also now recognise that by *not* doing the conventional thing and pursuing a 'black' vocal sound for whatever reason, both he and RORY MacDONALD have introduced something original to the rock repertoire – something identifiably Scottish – as well as something of incalculable value to Gaelic culture.

By 1976 or 1977 I was beginning to pay a bit more attention to the group. They still played a mixture of Scottish country dance and American country rock – and not terribly dynamically – but they were picking up a following in Skye, had made a Gaelic album and were talking of going full-time. This finally happened in 1979 and, by then, a metamorphosis had taken place. The accordion had been replaced by a rock guitarist who also played bagpipes and, in the wake of the 'punk' explosion, young Glasgow and Edinburgh Gaelic students and others were transforming their dances into clamouring, pogoing events.

This was the start of a career which was to scale heights unimaginable – at least to me – in the Portree days, but it was to these times and before, that I asked them to return when I interviewed Donnie, Rory and Calum MacDonald for *An Canan*, the arts supplement of the *West Highland Free Press*.

Both Rory and Calum spent their primary school years in North Uist:

RORY MacDONALD: 'The first music we were aware of was at our Granny's, listening to the Scottish and Irish requests on Radio Luxembourg: Bridie Gallagher and the

Gallowglas Ceilidh Band. Our grandmother came from Barra and was a great Flora MacNeill fan. The Mòd was followed every year on the radio and Angus McLeod, who's a cousin of our mother, made us aware of the great Uist singers. Also, of course, there was a lot of singing in the house, and our father always sang in the car.'

For Donnie, growing up in Portree, things were perceptibly different:

DONNIE MUNRO: 'There was not so much Gaelic in the village – people had often come there to work – but there was some great enthusiasts, and my mother sang a lot and was in choirs. She taught me a lot of songs like *The Glen Lyon Lament* which is on the first album. CALUM KENNEDY made a lot of impact on our lives and I would still have to list him as one of my favourite singers. I saw him in Portree Drill Hall.'

CALUM MacDONALD: 'We were in Portree by then *(1962/63)* and it was the first time I ever saw a guitar!'

DONNIE MUNRO: 'And PRESLEY . . . I remember my brother and I walked eight miles from the village of Treaslane where our grandparents lived, on a Saturday afternoon to see *Kid Galahad*. There were pictures on every Saturday night but no transport.'

Perhaps because he was the oldest, Rory was the one who made the earliest ventures into organised music.

RORY MacDONALD: 'I played accordion from about the age of seven and when I was 16 or 17 I was in a dance band called the SKYVERS. It was Scottish dance music with a difference and not dissimilar to what RUNRIG played when they started. No original material and no Gaelic – I had switched off Gaelic by then. Our big night was when the boxer, WALTER McGOWAN came to Broadford with CHRIS McLURE . . . he sang *Land Of A Thousand Dances* with us.'

DONNIE MUNRO: 'Calum and I were in the same class from Primary 5, and Blair *(Douglas)* was two years younger. I had been singing in local Mods and I won a silver medal, but never competed nationally. I had taken a scunner to the whole thing. When I started secondary school I became involved in folk groups, doing SIMON AND GARFUNKEL, DONOVAN and that sort of thing.'

CALUM MacDONALD: 'My motivation was because I was writing songs towards the end of school. I wasn't in any way musical, but the desire to write was very strong. Rory then went to art school in Glasgow and I followed him to do PE at Jordanhill.'

RORY MacDONALD: 'Blair's family had moved to Glasgow and they lived round the corner from our flat. We used to go there on Sunday nights for dinner. Blair was playing accordion by then and had been asked to play at a North Uist and Berneray gathering, upstairs in the Kelvin Hall. He suggested I play guitar, Calum came round with me and, while Blair and I worked out some chords, Calum was tapping his feet and playing with his hands on the table. Someone said, "What about a drummer?" Calum kept banging louder and louder and, next day, he was sent to Biggars shop to get a drum kit. Two weeks later we were playing!'

> The contrast between Calum's start as a drummer and that of some kids in the cities could not have been more marked. ROBBIE MacINTOSH *(of THE AVERAGE WHITE BAND)* for example, in Dundee, was playing along to BUDDY RICH records on a Ludwig drum kit at the age of 15. By the age of 18 he was touring Britain and Europe professionally, and before he was 20 – the same age at which Calum was starting – he was recording with top jazz/rock players such as Jim Mullen and Brian Auger.

RORY MacDONALD: 'We did that one date in Glasgow in April 1973 and it went down well, so we were encouraged to do some more in Skye.'

CALUM MacDONALD: 'The only place we could get was Waternish Hall. We booked six Friday or Saturday nights but only actually did one. It was just myself and Blair and must have been bloody awful! . . . but people invited us to play in Portree and Uig.'

> For Donnie, who was also home from art school in Edinburgh, a powerful shock was in store, and in more ways than one:

DONNIE MUNRO: 'One night, somebody said, "There's a band called RUNRIG playing," and I said, "Who's in that?" They said Blair, Rory and Calum MacDonald. I said "Rory's brother?" I had been right through school with Calum and never saw him hit an instrument or sing a song! I went up to the balcony at the Skye Gathering Hall and . . . I really enjoyed it! Hard, chunky Scottish dance music, and the vocal department was also interesting . . . *(great laughter)*.'

CALUM MacDONALD: 'I sang marginally worse than I played drums!'

DONNIE MUNRO: 'A few times then, I was at dances and I don't know if it was because I'd had a few drinks but, at the interval, I would go on with a guitar and sing with my cousin Monty playing drums. We did CORRIES songs and STATUS QUO and they then took me to Kyle as their support. I can't remember whether they asked me to join or if I suggested it.'

> FAIRPORT CONVENTION and what they had done with English folk music had made a big impression on the group and, even at that time, they had a kind of working philosophy.

RORY MacDONALD: 'The pop stuff was nowhere, but between Calum, Blair and myself there was a tremendous vibe for the Scottish stuff. Basically, we were a dance band, playing to excite people on the dance floor . . . then reacting to the audience. I moved back to Skye, and the summer of 1974 was the first full one we played.'

CALUM MacDONALD: 'We were at the transition from the community dances to the discos and dark halls. We still had to cater for everyone, though, and still played quicksteps.'

> BLAIR DOUGLAS was generally acknowledged as the musical virtuoso of the group, and left shortly afterwards to widen his musical horizons. His replacement was the late ROBERT MacDONALD, also from Skye, a first-class accordionist whose interest lay mainly in traditional music.

CALUM MacDONALD: 'We became more of a showband and had this double life . . . the band and the writing. Most of the songs were in English, but we hadn't the confidence to do them anyway . . . *then* I saw ANGUS MacLEOD again, singing at a wedding. I sat listening to him and was just knocked out. It was like Paul on the road to Damascus. Also, NA H'OGANAICH's first record had just come out and it provided a springboard for getting back into Gaelic. I remember going home and starting to write the first Gaelic song I'd ever written. It was a song I thought maybe Na h'Oganaich could record. Then we entered a song for the Killarney festival and it came second. It gave us confidence.'

178

RORY MacDONALD: 'The band had drifted by then. We had a house in Dalkeith and CAMPBELL GUNN and MACBEAT used to come out, and we mucked about with songs. It was out of all that that the Gaelic songs developed. Lismor was the only Gaelic label. We sent them four songs and they said, "Yes". The album was recorded and mixed in ten days on an 8-track, but we learned a lot.'

Left: BLAIR DOUGLAS
CAILEAN MACLEAN

Right: NA H'OGANAICH
GRAMPIAN TV

CAMPBELL GUNN was a singer/guitarist with the group NA SIARAICH. MacBeat is NEIL CAMPBELL, a virtuoso guitarist who was a contemporary of Rory's and went to London at a young age. At one point he auditioned for the JACK BRUCE BAND. Later he recorded and toured with the ELECTRIC CEILIDH BAND.

DONNIE MUNRO: 'The album was naïve, but the songs were good, and the important thing was, it was really exciting. I remember these journeys back and forth from Edinburgh to Glasgow. The feeling . . . bursting with excitement. After the record came out *(1977)*, we built it up. *Runrig's Return*. And in the summer of 1978 we arrived at the Skye Gathering Hall really full of enthusiasm . . . Gaelic Radio had been playing it . . . but we received the most hostile reaction. People

179

"What are you doing this crap for? . . . Who do you think you are?" And really, for a year we had to withstand lukewarm reaction and active hostility. In Lewis as well, because people were being faced with this mirror image which they were trying to get away from. It upset them. The real support came from Gaelic students based in the cities. They had obviously got this out of their system and were looking at Gaelic with a sense of pride.'

RORY MacDONALD: 'Robert wasn't so interested in the chosen *(rock)* direction, and Donnie had met MALCOLM JONES in Portree.'

DONNIE MUNRO: 'He was a piper and guitarist, and when he played with us, you could see the potential. He was at university and Blair had come back into the picture, and we decided to go full-time. A Grampian TV series came up – *Cuir Car* – and *Abisaidh* for BBC, so that enabled us to carry on. The National Mòd in Stornoway *(1979)* was then the real turning point.'

CALUM MacDONALD: 'That, and doing the song *Loch Lomond*.'

> It was certainly true that the availability of a media support system in the shape of Highland newspapers, radio in the Highlands and Islands and, in particular, Gaelic television was invaluable to the group, for it offered both exposure and much-needed financial sustenance at crucial stages. *Loch Lomond* was a song which all Scots could identify with, if not immediately endorse, and it became a kind of rallying song for the fans, in much the same way that the CORRIES are identified with *Flower Of Scotland*. Also, when it was re-recorded as a single it brought the group together with CHRIS HARLEY, a singer/songwriter who had settled in Skye, and whose production skills immediately improved their recorded performance and sound. The group was still compelled to handle its own affairs, however.

RORY MacDONALD: 'All the gigs, we promoted ourselves. We couldn't get into universities and promoters like George Duffin wouldn't have anything to do with us. So we did everything ourselves . . . bookings, flyposting.'

DONNIE MUNRO: 'One amusing story . . . We did the first big Plaza *(Ballroom)* night and billed it "Celtic Rock Night". We were flyposting at Bridgeton Cross late at night *(Rangers territory)* . . . these guys came along and said, "Ho! What the f— is this Celtic music by the way?" "K," we said, trying not to panic, "It's Keltic."'

Major gambles had to be taken where recording was concerned, as well. *Highland Connection*, the first album in the rock idiom, cost them £8,000 to make, and *Recovery* twice that, at a time when the group had reverted to part-time work. It was, however, a more assured album artistically, and produced by Robert Bell of the BLUE NILE. Their sound was beginning to take shape and the new confidence led to a decision to give up day jobs once and for all and sign with an English Independent record label – Simple Records. The move was almost catastrophic and at one point led to the farcical allegation of chart-hyping of singles. The notion was ridiculous as they, probably more than any other group in the UK, suffered from a Gallup system which only sampled in major centres, since the group sold large numbers of records in rural outlets.

NEIL CAMPBELL

N. CAMPBELL

DONNIE MUNRO: 'They virtually cleaned us out. There was no financial input and two days before we were due to go into the studio, we got a phone call saying there was no money. We had been off the road to rehearse and previously, two promoters had managed to lose us money on a sell-out tour . . .'

CALUM MacDONALD: 'So *Heartland* was the biggest gamble of all.'

RORY MacDONALD: 'We carried on with the recording and were getting phone calls: "Such and such a *(merchant)* bank has turned us down." We were only looking for guarantors, and latterly we got a commitment from *Comunn na Gaidhlig* and people who had worked in the business with us.'

DONNIE MUNRO: 'Things changed when Marlene Ross came in as manager *(1983)*. She formalised our finances and learned quickly from the Simple thing. *Heartland* recovered its money within a year.'

> And to what extent can Gaelic music continue to find a place in the US-dominated market-place?

DONNIE MUNRO: 'The whole thing about commerciality is *access*. If enough people get access, they'll decide whether they want it or not. What is available through major radio stations is so narrow, it's bound to nurture a limited public taste.

I recently asked my wee girl aged ten, who her favourite singer was. She said, "Roy Orbison".'

181

DONNIE MUNRO &
RUNRIG CHRYSALIS
RECORDS *Inset:*
MARLENE ROSS
M. ROSS

MARLENE ROSS

'Not your normal manager'

It is a well-worn cliché that behind every successful man is a woman, so I suppose it should come as no surprise to find an extraordinary woman behind the extraordinary success of the group RUNRIG. Born and brought up in Aberdeen, MARLENE ROSS retains her business base there, dividing her time between two sons aged 18 and 21, and managing the music-business phenomenon which the Skye group has become.

'I was never really that interested in music when I was younger,' she says. 'I went to Aberdeen Folk Club and later my husband had discos, but all I ever really wanted to be was a nurse.'

Marlene's mother came from the city but I suspect her roots are really in rural Aberdeenshire, on the Deeside, where her father's family had a little croft and shoemaker's shop. She herself grew up in the West End of Aberdeen and attended Kaimhill school.

'I trained at Aberdeen Royal Infirmary and did my midwifery at Glasgow's Rotten Row. Then I came back to Aberdeen and when I was made Theatre Sister I was the youngest nurse ever to be promoted to such a position in Scotland. I was 21.'

Marlene continued nursing for another four years, then gave it up to have a family. With her husband's disco business developing, however, they decided to open a music shop which would try to cater for the specialist technical needs of local musicians. Soon she was engrossed in the business of Abbotsford Acoustics.

'We helped a number of Aberdeen groups at this time, just on a personal basis, and did some promoting at Ritzy's. Although I still wasn't that involved, I could see that the musicians were making an awful lot of mistakes. I began trying to steer them in the right direction, get the right fees, and so forth.

The first time I heard of RUNRIG they phoned from Skye to hire a PA for one of their own promotions at the Douglas Hotel, Aberdeen. No one had really heard of them here and I didn't even bother going! Anyway, we got the folk singer LES HONEYMAN to hire them a half-decent PA and it was Les who later suggested that they approach me for management. This would have been in the late Seventies.

I went to see them at Aberdeen University Union and really fell in love with their music. Donnie's voice I always thought was brilliant, the songs were good and they were getting a bit of reaction, but they weren't very professional. I invited them back to Aberdeen for a meeting. They said they wanted to go full-time, but had commitments, and wondered if I could keep them in wages. I had never done anything like that – trying to find £700 or £800 every week – but they were keen and we decided to try.'

> Marlene herself had no doubts that she could cope with the new situation on a personal level.

'The nursing training was the best training in the world. You are absolutely disciplined and trained to deal with any kind of emergency. I therefore know how to handle people psychologically – especially when they start cracking up! Promoters, crew, etc – that's my forté. I never, ever lose my temper.'

With the band, relations were always built on trust:

'When I met them first of all, I just fell in love with them all. They were so honest, sincere and up-front. I like to think I'm that type of person myself, but I didn't come into contact with it much, down here. Everyone was more streetwise and "wide". I was under surveillance myself, of course, but in business I was much less naïve than the band. One of the first things I did was ask Ian Bayne, who was still drumming with the group, NEW CELESTE, to make a choice.'

> Such simple but effective decision-making got things off to a good start, although the band had to be taken off the road for a while so that Marlene could hold out for the necessary (higher) fees. The relationship was soon to suffer a setback, however, when the group was approached by, and decided to go along with, two Glasgow-based promoters who offered to handle a single *(Loch Lomond)* and their next Scottish tour.

'They were music-business types which I was not, and offering Scottish tour assistance which I did not think the group needed. I sat at home and cried. I sent them a telegram which said "I'm with you in spirit", but I was dead against the whole operation and, in a sense was proved right. There was also a record deal with a London-based independent – Simple Records – who tried to take away artistic control from the band – and, all in all, it was the most catastrophic time.

The band wasn't ready for a deal. They went about with their leads in carrier bags and still had a lot of building-up to do. What we had to do was move at our own pace, getting the artwork right and the production as good as possible and – most important – *retaining total control.*'

The title of the previous record album – *Recovery* – had perhaps been more pertinent than was anticipated. For the next two years it was the group who were recovering.

'*Heartland* was the most difficult album to make because we found it so hard to finance. The bank in Portree was supportive, but not the head office and, in the end, it was really down to friends and relatives. For a short period they had to go on to lower wages and I, of course, was taking nothing. We still had the shop.

The band, however, was fundamentally different from other groups. It had obvious qualities of honesty and sincerity which others didn't, and slowly, record companies and others began to come round. There just seemed to be a turning point – when the time was right, if you like – and we signed with Chrysalis in 1987.

When I went to London at first there were very few companies I could have worked with. I was amazed at the type of people who held high positions and I wasn't impressed. It was all fashion, and we weren't about that at all. Chrysalis were different . . . decent people with continuity of staff. I also took advice from music business solicitors although, being a typical Scot, I still had my Scottish solicitor checking everything! Solo *(the London agency)* have also helped, both with the record deal and by insisting that we keep our own Scottish promotions.'

Marlene tells a story which is typical of her no-nonsense approach, and how it frequently gets results:

'John Giddings *(Solo)* always reminds me of how he first enquired about being RUNRIG's agent. He phoned up and said, "Would you like to come to see us in London?" I said, "Look, the band is playing at Eden Court in Inverness. Get your arses up here!"'

I would love to have seen their faces when first confronted by Marlene's style, but I have no doubt that she now enjoys the respect of both record company and agency executives. Her logic is quite simple:

'I'm not known in the business as the softest person that walks around, but that is

185

people who don't know me. In a way I'm very soft, but it is a hard business so I have to give a hard image. I've got to go in, not aggressively, but in a determined way or I'd get trampled underfoot.'

For the future it will be more of the same.

'I've never seen anything as instant. I see it as a working thing, building steadily. Beyond that, I'd like to see Scotland managed better!'

RUNRIG CDC LEISURE SERVICES

Marlene Ross is not talking about football.

CHAPTER TWENTY-FOUR

JOHN MARTYN

'I was going to be a doctor . . .'

JOHN MARTYN is a consummate musician whose folk/jazz blues guitar and vocal style has been admired and copied at home and abroad for more than 20 years. At the time of writing he was recording his twenty-eighth album – most of which have appeared on the Island label. He was born Iain David McGeachy in 1948.

'I was actually born in New Malden in Surrey. Both my parents were professional *JOHN MARTYN* singers: my father was "Scotland's Troubadour" – Russell Paterson, and my mother's professional name was Betty Benson. She came from Belgium and separated from my father when I was eight months old.

My father's family came from Kintyre and I still have people there. My father grew up in Campbeltown and Edinburgh and then his mother moved to Shawlands in Glasgow which is where I was brought up. It was a fairly big house with pianos in just about every room and all my aunts and uncles would gather round the piano in that Victorian tradition and sing and play. Songs like *Down By The Salley Gardens, Mairi's Wedding* and *I Know Where I'm Going.*

I briefly took up violin but they took the piss out of me in the rugby team and, as the lessons coincided with the circuit training, that was it . . . they had to go. I was never any good at it anyway and I didn't enjoy it. This was at Shawlands Academy.

I was a late starter on guitar *(16)*. I hung around as a sort of apprentice to HAMISH IMLACH for a year and a half and learned from that. I met him through a friend of my father's – Billy Synott – who was interested in socialist politics and loved folk clubs. He liked CISCO HOUSTON and WOODY GUTHRIE and that's how I got into the bluesier aspect of folk music. Also Hamish in these days played almost exclusively blues, very little traditional stuff.

I was interested in the black angle of things . . . BLIND BLAKE, BLIND LEMON JEFFERSON, BUKKA WHITE, and I seemed to pick up the styles really easily. I had always had an ear, playin' the moothie and that, and within a year I was makin' money. I sometimes played at the Glasgow Folk Centre – BILLY CONNOLLY was there at that time and ALEX HARVEY and his brother – and it was run by a guy called Andrew Moyes who used to charge me ten bob to sing three songs!

The wider pop thing didn't make that much of an impression on me. The

BEATLES were played at parties and I would go dancing on a Friday but my girlfriend had to be in by eleven, so, on the Saturday, I would then go up to Clive's Incredible Folk Club in Sauchiehall Street. This was Clive Palmer who became a member of the INCREDIBLE STRING BAND and that's how they got their name. People sometimes forget that it was originally his band. I picked up everything there . . . but I never considered music as a career. I was going to be a doctor.

All my father's family were both intelligent and musical. My aunt taught music and all my cousins are bright. One's a geologist, one's actually a brain surgeon . . . and it was a good educational system at that time. I got nine 'A' levels and went to Cambridge University to do medicine. I felt out of place, though, and I didn't like it. Still don't. Too snobbish. My accent wasn't "right", I didn't have the correct manners . . . a different background altogether.

Anyway, I was into my first year and living in Kingston-on-Thames. I had got into the habit of playin' at folk clubs and sounded competent because I had discovered open tunings – I still play in one particular one – and this was the key to my original material which I was writing from the very first. This fella came up to me in a club . . . his name was Theo Johnston . . . and said, "Excuse me, but I can make you a star. I know this guy, Chris Blackwell, who has a new record company, Island Records." I was 18 and just lucky. On the Saturday night I was heard in a folk club. By the Wednesday I had done the deal and by the Thursday I was in a wee studio cutting an album! Chris had tiny offices in Oxford Street and Kilburn and I recorded *London Conversations* on a Revox in Putney. There was no white music on Island at that time, apart from *Bawdy Ballads,* Volumes I and II – dirty songs sung by rugby teams! Then Millie had her hit with *My Boy Lollipop* and that was how Chris began to get the capital to develop the company.

He liked a song of mine called *Fairy Tale Lullaby* and wanted it as a single but I had never been in a studio before and it didn't quite go the way he wanted it. Anyway, I had been at Cambridge for four and a half months and the family were horrified at my leaving. But as soon as I got the offer to play, I was away.

The first two albums were folky – the STRING BAND had been a big influence – then I heard THE BAND and that influenced the next two albums, *Stormbringer* and *Road To Ruin*. I actually went to the States and recorded with LEVON HELM and RICK DANKO.

Then I became interested in jazz. The production company I was working with had another band with Cuban percussion and Puerto Rican influences . . . a bit like SANTANA . . . and by then I felt I had the guitar-playing down. I was also listening to Indian and North African music and Bulgarian stuff and the *Solid Air* album came around this time *(early Seventies)*. It sold something in excess of 100,000 copies and paid my debts with Island. Also the song *May You Never* came from this album and has done well over the years.

Then came the reggae stuff, but I was overworking, overdrinking, overdrugging and scunnered with life in general and Chris suggested I go to Jamaica to try and refresh myself. I did a lot of work with LEE "SCRATCH" PERRY, BURNING SPEAR and MAX ROMEO and I lived at Strawberry Hill but, if you got paid at all it was in dodgy dollars or blue movies. It could be a wild place. I covered *Johnny Too Bad* by JOHNNY AND THE SHOOTOUTS – all of whom were later shot in different incidents!

Around that time I developed a great interest in the work of JOE ZAWINUL and WEATHER REPORT. I just fell in love with that whole area and I think my new album has some of that influence. Curiously, JONI MITCHELL, who also worked in open tunings, went the same way, developing an interest in jazz, although I think it was the accessibility of her singles which gave her a wider audience.

I've toured the States a dozen times, twice with a band, and I've worked with a number of the top jazz people, mainly at the Bijou Club in Philadelphia, but I never felt the desire to push fully into jazz. I think you need a lot of technical knowledge and I still play by ear!

On the question of Scottish music . . . I've experimented with some Scottish stuff but I've been quoted as saying that I consider myself a citizen of the world and I did an album called *One World*. Having said that, I love Scots and Irish music and it may be partisan but I do consider that they take a great deal of care over their music. Perhaps more so than the English. I loved MOVING HEARTS, for example.

After Jamaica, I came back to Hastings and, in the late Seventies, I moved back to Scotland to look after my father. Annie and I have been in the Borders since 1983 and I've been working with bands consistently since that period – and before. The first one was with ALAN THOMSON, JIM PRIME and JEFF ALLEN. Then there was one with FOSS PATERSON and COLIN TULLY. And the current album has JOE LOCKE from the States on vibes, SPENCER COZENS *(keyboards)*, and DAVE LEWIS *(sax)* with ANDY SHEPHARD *(sax)* guesting.

As I say, I've been quite lucky in the music business. I had one huge court case with a former manager, Sandy Robertson – again, Chris Blackwell bailed me out, to Nassau this time – but even in the music business, you can withdraw your labour. I've come unstuck a couple of times but, basically, I've battled through the wind.'

EPILOGUE

'World Music' is how EDWYN COLLINS describes rock'n'roll . . . 'the music of poor immigrants'. I find this as acceptable a way as any of explaining why young people throughout the world identify with its musical and emotional qualities although these are frequently expressed in unfamiliar cultural terms. The notion of displacement would therefore seem central to the rhythm and blues or rock'n'roll theme and, even within the context of contemporary urban Scotland, the musical contribution of the migrant or immigrant – Irish, Highland, Italian – is never far from the surface.

It is black American music, however, which appears to have been the most enduring Scottish passion. Whenever I hear the early Sixties JAMES BROWN song *Please, Please, Please*, I think of Scottish teenagers awakening to black music. I don't particularly like the song – at the time I was much more keen on *Out Of Sight* or *Papa's Got A Brand New Bag*, not to mention OTIS REDDING or WILSON PICKETT – but there is something about the background voices on *Please, Please, Please* which always reminds me of the fascination I had when I first heard black music: resonant, mature voices with a hint of desperation and from an apparently exotic culture which was not shown on American films or TV. Everything therefore had to be imagined which, of course, served to heighten the effect.

The impact of this music on a country, drab and muted by the hangover of war, was tremendous. The first problem was getting to hear more of it and DOUG MARTIN talks of the frustration of hearing an exciting song on the radio and having to wait for weeks to hear it again.

Then you had to find a place that sold the record. GRAHAM LYLE had to locate a Teddy Boy in the basement of a hardware shop. ALEX HARVEY looked to a merchant seaman, home from the Caribbean.

Acquiring and learning an instrument has historically shown evidence of ingenious solutions to apparently insurmountable problems. Tea chests and Dettol cans have been requisitioned; embryonic guitarists in the Seventies, like their skiffle predecessors, were forced to improvise upon ukuleles; and rehearsals were always problematic. In living rooms, up closes – the task was as great a test of pragmatism and creativity as the crafting of original songs.

Then came the first gigs. Some, as in black or Italian America, happened on street corners. The early importance of organisations like the church, the youth club, the Boys Brigade and Scouts is restated again and again and, thereafter, the cultural benefits of Highland dance hall circuits in the north and miners' clubs in the south, are manifest. It is significant, for example, that the first BEATLES tour *anywhere* incorporated gigs from both territories – Elgin, for example, and Alloa – and other mining areas like Rosewell near Edinburgh, Sauchie in Clackmannan, Ayrshire and Kirkcaldy get regular mentions. This may also be the underlying reason why Dunfermline and Lanarkshire have particularly interesting musical traditions and the Dundee soul music scene merits a study in its own right. Whilst on the subject of geography, is it not incredible that bands have made such determined efforts to reach Caithness, Orkney and Shetland since earliest times? And these areas have, of course, also produced some fine bands of their own.

The role of urban gangs in Scottish youth culture appears to parallel that of the music groups over decades and particularly in Glasgow where the gang leaders seemed to identify with the local pop stars. Drink is reluctant to relinquish its status as the most popular Scottish drug and sectarianism would appear to be alive and well, at least in the west. Racism and sexism, however, are not readily apparent in the Scottish music business. Political issues in general, in fact, are not very high on the agenda although they have had a higher profile in recent years and traditional Scottish socialist analysis is common both to Labourites and Nationalists.

Although I know about it at first-hand, the sheer hard work involved in the music profession comes across in these interviews. ALAN DARBY's tale of collecting a hired car at 7 a.m., rounding-up the band, and driving to London, helping to set up the gear, performing, packing the gear away and driving back to Glasgow will be a story not entirely unfamiliar to generations of Scottish musicians and reflecting upon the nine years of PETE AGNEW's life which have been spent on tour in America is a sobering thought, not least for his wife and family. And now he's off to Eastern Europe! Little wonder that GRAHAM LYLE's son did not recognise his father or that DOUG MARTIN felt like 'just going away and being "normal" for a while'.

In general terms, the professional female musicians interviewed appear to have had a greater concern with actual musicality than their male counterparts and tend to come from more established family musical traditions. Perhaps it is more difficult for the untrained woman to make her mark in the rough and tumble. And both men and women entering the profession seem to be better qualified educationally nowadays. The perennial parental guidance of 'getting something behind you first' seems to be getting across although, at the time of writing, MICHAEL MARRA still has no 'O' levels.

Two things became obvious in the wake of the BEATLES' international success. One, that marketing a good image was vitally important and this was brilliantly exploited by TAM PATON and the BAY CITY ROLLERS and, later, by ANNIE LENNOX; and two, that quality original material was essential. JACK BRUCE, the AVERAGE WHITE BAND and GRAHAM LYLE were the first Scots to achieve sustained impact in this area although it was only possible because they were prepared to commit themselves to living and working in London and, sometimes, America.

The move to London has been more than just a train of thought for Scots musicians over the years. Until the Eighties the absence of record companies and recording studios was a severe handicap to all the regions and, although the major companies have yet to see the light and establish offices outside the metropolis, there are now a number of top class studios and good, independent record labels in Scotland. Indeed, the early success of RUNRIG was facilitated by the existence of a healthy, independent, Gaelic record market which had been built up over decades and Scots indies have now come together in the Scottish Record Industry Association with the avowed intention of establishing a Scottish chart and a more vigorous indigenous record scene.

The factors which did most to transform the relationship between Scotland and the popular music industry were the advent of punk music and the social, artistic and business attitudes which it encouraged (they had existed to a minor degree in Scotland before) – the so-called post-punk ethic. Although, as EDWYN COLLINS has again pointed out, punk was largely the creation of middle-class art students, like football – in the words of journalist Jack MacLean – it was soon appropriated by the dispossessed and this led to the development of independent record companies and putative management structures throughout the regions. The grip of the multi-national record companies and music papers was then briefly loosened and this gave potential managers such as Bruce Findlay *(SIMPLE MINDS)*, Alan Horne *(ORANGE JUICE)*, Elliot Davis *(WET WET WET)*, Alan MacNeill *(HUE AND CRY)*, and Kenny MacDonald *(PROCLAIMERS)* valuable breathing space in which to make the unavoidable errors which an apprenticeship entails. The emergence of similarly successful women in this area (Marlene Ross, Gill Maxwell) is also a significant and healthy development.

Perhaps something should also be said about the importance of the dole (unemployment benefit) to musicians and the music scene as a whole. It is undeniable that such civilised legislation has been crucial to the economic survival of generations of young musicians and would-be managers as they built up their marketing base and the investment has frequently paid the state off handsomely in terms of taxation, job creation and so forth.

At the time of writing, new Tory rules concerning job training and unemployment benefit appear to be making life at the subsistence level more difficult for many young people.

Of the music itself, Scotland has produced many top-class instrumentalists but quality singers above all and a particularly good batch seems to have come along at the same time in the Eighties: ANNIE LENNOX, EDDI READER, RICKY ROSS, MARTI PELLOW, PAT KANE to name but a few, plus some exceptional young writers like PAUL BUCHANAN and GARY CLARKE. For that reason alone it is not difficult to understand why Glasgow became highly fashionable around the middle of the 1980s. The role of journalists in this process should not be underestimated, as more and more young Scots began to gain access to the national press in an attempt to describe the developing phenomenon.

I have left the question of Scottish or indigenous rock music until last because I feel that this is the key to the future of popular music in Scotland and, indeed, throughout the world. Scotland is uniquely poised. We have absorbed black musical influences over a period of decades and taken those cultures to our heart in a way that must be beneficial to Scottish society as a whole. Taking that as our baseline, what we must now do is focus upon those other exotic cultures as defined by the Gaelic and Scots languages, those geographically and educationally isolated cultures to which media access has traditionally been restricted and which divest their rich musical traditions with the same enthusiasm and creative energy.

Some major Scottish artistes such as DEACON BLUE have now taken tentative steps in this area and others, like MICHAEL MARRA, the PROCLAIMERS and RUNRIG have made real headway. The phenomenal success of RUNRIG in Scotland itself has highlighted the latent interest in, and commercial potential of Gaelic crossover. The language itself is often perceived by Scots as difficult but, with increased educational and media access and possibly broadcasting/governmental infrastructural support (such as a dedicated recording studio) more musicians and listeners may be able to explore the delights of Gaelic song and poetry.

The Scots language has slightly different problems in the context of rock music: a combination of range of sounds (in this respect it is more limited than Gaelic yet, paradoxically, more expressive than English) and image. The fact that mid-Atlantic sounding Scots have long been considered figures of fun in this country does the musical cause no favours.

Like Gaelic, Scots has been handicapped in educational and media terms but the PROCLAIMERS and others have shown that it can work commercially in the crossover context and I feel that aesthetic enhancement will come at the point where Scots language rock'n'rollers meet the more traditional Scottish folk artistes who themselves continue to experiment with electric instruments and American structures.

It should perhaps also be said that in no way do I envisage any kind of electric crossover music – rock'n'roll or whatever – somehow replacing traditional music. Perish the thought. It is, however, a musical adjunct of such global and commercial importance, its artistic refinement and success could not fail to have positive repercussions upon the indigenous folk music and cultures of Scotland.